T0030301

NORTH CAROLINA
IN THE

NORTH CAROLINA
IN THE

1950s

THE **DECADE**
IN **MOTION**

PHILIP GERARD

BLAIR

Blair is an imprint of Carolina Wren Press.

CWP

*The mission of Blair/Carolina Wren Press is to seek out, nurture, and
promote literary work by new and underrepresented writers.*

We gratefully acknowledge the ongoing support of general operations
by the Durham Arts Council's United Arts Fund
and the North Carolina Arts Council.

Designed by Miranda Young

ISBN: 978-1-949467-92-5
Library of Congress Control Number: 2022945326

ALSO BY PHILIP GERARD

The Art of Creative Research

Cape Fear Rising

Down the Wild Cape Fear:
A River Journey Through the Heart of North Carolina

The Dark of the Island

Hatteras Light

The Last Battleground:
The Civil War Comes to North Carolina

The Patron Saint of Dreams

Things We Do When No One Is Watching

North Carolina in the 1940s: The Decade of Transformation

CONTENTS

CONTENTS

THE **DECADE** IN **MOTION**

The war is fading from memory, the boys are long home, and people are moving quickly and optimistically toward a bright future. There is movement everywhere—literal movement on the minor league baseball diamonds of the Piedmont and coastal plain, on the streamlined trains and airliners carrying passengers en masse between cities, on the highways crowded with a parade of big, brightly painted automobiles with plush upholstery and powerful motors. The Sunday drive now becomes a family outing with no particular destination, the trip itself an event, the automobile the new emblem of freedom and mobility.[1]

With gas rationing a thing of the past, during the postwar boom the automobile comes into its own. Three new national defense interstates, I-85, I-95, and I-40, take shape and advance into North Carolina—hundreds of miles of fast, four-lane freeways. Simultaneously, the state undertakes an ambitious program to extend and modernize its farm-to-market roads— thousands of miles of new roads are built, and other routes are upgraded for all-weather travel. By mid-decade, these new highways support the fourth largest trucking industry in the nation, home to more Class I motor carriers—tractor trailers—than any other state.

And two new phenomena seem to bloom out of the landscape overnight: the drive-in movie theater and the drive-in restaurant.

Automobiles bring tourists to the coast and the mountain counties—the auto vacation is the new luxury. Grandfather Mountain, privately owned by the Hugh MacRae family, has long been a star attraction for tourists visiting the high country around Linville, Blowing Rock, Banner Elk, and Boone. Hugh Morton, MacRae's grandson, inherits the property and begins working to make it more accessible—widening the climbing

Familiar sights: the Mile-High Swinging Bridge at Grandfather Mountain became an instant tourist attraction when it opened in 1952.

trail and building the most famous bridge in the state at its summit—a 228-foot-long suspension bridge popularly called the Mile-High Swinging Bridge.

Morton, a conservationist and accomplished photographer, acts as a steward of the property, preserving its natural features and documenting its breathtaking vistas in his photographs. His mother, Agnes MacRae Morton, and Donald MacDonald cofound the Highland Games and bring the annual event to the mountain.[2]

While the automobile is beginning to crowd out rail travel, for the time being passengers can still enjoy a fast and luxurious ride on two rival carriers—the Atlantic Coast Line Railroad and the Seaboard Air Line Railroad—aboard streamlined trains pulled by purple, silver, yellow, green, and orange locomotives with names like *Champion* and *Orange Blossom Special.*[3]

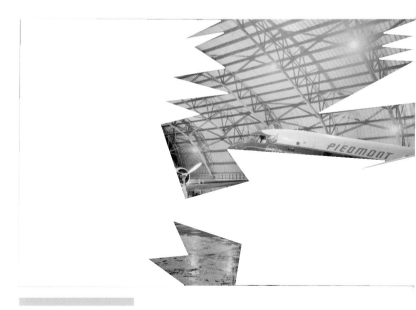

Piedmont Airlines' DC-3s were icons of the skies above North Carolina.

And Piedmont Airlines, which launches its first flight from Wilmington to Cincinnati just before the decade turns, offers city-to-city service on its fleet of sleek silver, blue, and white DC-3 aircraft: New Bern to Louisville, Kentucky; Asheville to Roanoke, Virginia; and longer flights to Washington, D.C., and other big cities.[4]

On a tract of land just north of Carolina Beach, stretching from the Cape Fear River across the peninsula to Myrtle Grove Sound, Black families find entertainment and music. Segregation prohibits them from white hotels and clubs. Besides the resort hotels on the water, more than thirty juke joints offer dancing to the hottest numbers played on a jukebox. Some, like Jitterbug Johnnie's, book live bands that play bebop, boogie, and swing music long into the night for the crowds of fashionably dressed dancers.

While Black and white audiences are separated by law, their music is not. Carolina Beach juke joint owners soon stock the so-called race records, and "beach music" takes hold among white teenagers—a crossover music style that sets the stage for rock 'n' roll. They dance exuberantly on sawdusted juke joint dance floors at Seabreeze and Carolina Beach, young couples—Black and white—swinging to the hot new sounds of Black entertainers like Amos Milburn, Paul Williams, and Count Basie.[5]

The Civil Rights movement carries the state inexorably into the future. Many of its decisive moments play out in North Carolina. In 1951, following a court order, the University of North Carolina opens its graduate and professional schools to Black students.[6]

In 1954, the U.S. Supreme Court orders all public schools desegregated—but in North Carolina, the legislature's Pearsall Committee concocts a plan to "moderate" the process, declaring in its report, "The mixing of the races in the public schools within the state cannot be accomplished and should not be attempted."[7]

Nonetheless, a handful of Black students enroll in Charlotte, Greensboro, and Winston-Salem. Black parents in Durham file suit to allow their children to be admitted to the all-white high school. Meanwhile, seven Black protesters occupy the white section of a Durham ice cream shop and are arrested. In February 1960, a year after Dr. Martin Luther King delivers an inspiring speech in Greensboro, the tension comes to a head when four students from North Carolina Agricultural and Technical College stage a sit-in at the Woolworth's lunch counter there—and this new, effective form of protest is emulated by other activists across the South. In North Carolina, the Civil Rights movement takes on new urgency and vigor.[8]

In Robeson County, in the southeastern corner of the state, the Lumbee Indians have long sought tribal recognition. Their origin is poorly documented, and some already recognized tribes place doubts on the Lumbees' descent—despite the findings of an anthropologist from the Smithsonian Institution who studied the tribe in the 1930s: he declared they are of Siouan (Cheraw and Keyauwee) origin. Once known as the Croatan—after the Indians who lived on Roanoke Island when it was colonized by the English—in 1913 they were redesignated as the Cherokee Indians of Robeson County.

At last, in 1953, the state legislature recognizes them as the Lumbee—the tribe's chosen name.[9]

The Lumbee continue to suffer harassment, notably from the Ku Klux Klan. In 1958, led by Wizard James "Catfish" Cole, the Klan stages a torchlit rally outside Maxton. Hundreds of Lumbee Indians, many of them armed, descend on the rally and chase the Klan from the area in what becomes nationally famous as the Battle of Hayes Pond.[10]

The University of North Carolina moves to extend its educational reach across the entire state by taking its mission to the airwaves.

Through the visionary work of UNC's chief finance officer, William C. "Billy" Carmichael, Kay Kyser (a renowned big-band leader), and William C. Friday, WUNC-TV Channel 4 in Chapel Hill goes on the air, backed by a small appropriation from the legislature and $1.8 million raised from individuals, corporations, and foundations. Its inaugural broadcast, on January 8, 1955, features a basketball twin bill between UNC-Chapel Hill and Wake Forest.

Friday, assistant to the president of the consolidated UNC campus, hosts *North Carolina People*, which becomes the station's signature—and longest running—show. Friday himself becomes president of UNC in 1956 and remains true to his goal of extending the broadcast reach to all one hundred counties.[11]

In downtown Raleigh, the North Carolina Museum of Art opens on Morgan Street in 1956, occupying the former State Highway Division building. The museum is made possible by an unprecedented act of cultural awareness: in 1947, the legislature appropriated $1 million to purchase 139 American and European works of art for the people of North Carolina—supplemented by seventy-one additional works acquired by the Samuel H. Kress Foundation. It's the first major collection in the country to be funded by a state government. The museum signals a civic commitment to the cultural heritage of the state, a recognition that such heritage is tied fast to educational and economic progress.[12]

With the scaling down of shipyards and other wartime industries, the state actively recruits new industry—textile and tobacco are historically low-paying enterprises, and to prosper,

North Carolina needs industries that can offer higher wages and attract educated young workers—too many of whom are out-migrating to more lucrative opportunities elsewhere. The notion of a research center partnered with leading universities is first floated by Howard Odum, a University of North Carolina at Chapel Hill sociologist, in 1952. An industry-recruitment delegation representing the state includes Romeo Guest, a builder and MIT graduate from Greensboro.

A look at the map reveals a triangle of farmland and pine forest formed in the space between Raleigh, Durham, and Chapel Hill—each point anchored by a major research university—and Guest coins the term *Research Triangle*. With leadership from the universities and business executives such as Archibald Davis of Wachovia Bank, by the end of 1959, the nonprofit Research Triangle Park is home to five companies acting in partnership with university researchers, moving the state to the forefront of entrepreneurial innovation.[13]

W. Kerr Scott wins election to the governorship at the turn of the decade with his slogan, "Go Forward." In his inaugural address, he proposes to use the state budget surplus to propel North Carolina toward transformational public improvements. By the end of his four years in office in 1953, he reports on just how much progress has "gone forward": many new schools and a statewide school health program; new hospitals and a more comprehensive public health program; seventy-five thousand new telephone installations in rural areas, along with thousands more homes electrified; thousands of miles of new paved secondary roads; and modern deepwater ports established at Wilmington and Morehead City.[14]

Scott is succeeded by William B. Umstead, who suffers a heart attack just two days after his inauguration and dies in 1954. Lt. Gov. Luther Hartwell Hodges, now chief executive, continues Scott's agenda and energetically supports the creation of Research Triangle Park.

Some of the movement of the '50s is retrograde, as the struggle for civil rights fuels a backlash in the streets and in the legislature. But in general North Carolina reshapes itself as a much more urbanized state (all that movement to the cities), and the population grows, even as out-migration increases—ambitious people taking advantage of their postwar freedom to seek better wages and more equitable working conditions in more progressive states.

By decade's end, the state has reshaped itself on the foundation laid by the frenetic prosperity of the war years. It remains a work in progress—and that is its defining feature: *progress*.

Along the Carolina coast, beach music evolved from dance records popular at Black resorts like Seabreeze.

CHAPTER

SEABREEZE: RHYTHM AND BEACH MUSIC

The seeds of a new, high-energy dance music were planted in the 1940s on a tract of land just north of Carolina Beach, stretching from the river across the peninsula to Myrtle Grove Sound in a lively resort community called Seabreeze. Now as the decade turns, it becomes the destination of choice for Black families from near and far. Segregation still prohibits Black patrons from white hotels and clubs, such as those in Wilmington and at Wrightsville Beach to the north. Seabreeze becomes not just a wildly popular haven for Black families seeking leisure but also a place that transforms the musical soundscape of the South—and the nation.

A hundred years earlier, Alexander and Charity Freeman, "free colored persons," acquired about 180 coastal acres. Their son, Robert Bruce Freeman, illiterate but shrewd in business, acquired more land at the going rate of fifteen cents per acre—including Gander Hall Plantation and Sedgeley Abbey Plantation with its magisterial mansion—a total of 2,500 acres. Eventually he held more than 5,000 acres. He donated land for a school and a church campground, attracting as many as 3,000 people to a camp meeting.[1]

Later generations of Freemans farmed the land and fished the waters offshore, mined clay and granite, harvested timber, and distilled whiskey. And they intentionally worked to turn the waterfront acreage to viable commercial enterprises. Gradually the ocean beach and inshore land became a place where Black people could swim, dine, and dance without interference from their white neighbors.[2]

In 1913, some of the heirs sold a tract just south, on the north boundary of Carolina Beach, and when those seaside lots were sold, Black people were prohibited from buying them—thus eventually hemming in the Freeman beach property without its own road access. Visitors would have to swim the narrow sound or wade across to the ocean beach at low tide—or be ferried in small boats.[3]

Meanwhile, cottages sprang up—not just rude structures but attractive upscale bungalows described by a Harlem-based columnist as "swank," occupied by "a sporting crowd dressed in linen suits and driving roadsters." In 1922, Tom and Victoria Lofton of Wilmington opened the Russell Hotel at Seabreeze, a three-story resort offering twenty-five airy rooms, a restaurant, and, perhaps most important, a dance hall, inaugurated with a performance by Frank Herring's seven-piece orchestra.[4]

Farther up the coast, in 1924, Thomas H. Wright and Charles B. Parmele established a competing Black resort on Shell Island, just north of Wrightsville Beach, with a pavilion, bathhouse, restaurant, pier, and 274 platted lots for building along fourteen streets. A ferry made four round trips daily to and from the barrier island. Thousands gathered for its grand opening, and visitors arrived from as far away as New York and Alabama. The promoters described the project as not just a resort but "a movement founded in the forethought of liberal businessmen of the south who realize that the Negro's outlet for social and recreational development has heretofore been severely limited."[5]

But Shell Island survived just three summers before its main buildings were destroyed by a spate of suspicious fires "of undetermined origin"—likely arson. Investors abandoned the ruined resort in 1926. Wrightsville Beach officials then passed

A couple embraces on a North Carolina beach.

ordinances restricting Black bathers to the northernmost tip of the beach and prohibited them from even promenading on the boardwalk, where they could be seen from white-owned cottages. Seabreeze became an even more prominent leisure haven for the Black community, and in the 1920s, Ellis Freeman sold lots that offered full access to the beach and encouraged Black entrepreneurs to set up restaurants and hotels. By the 1930s, Seabreeze was going strong.[6]

A decade later, it counted three hotels and ten restaurants, including Sadie Wade's, which specialized in deep-fried clam fritters that sold for a nickel apiece. Seabreeze also had a bingo parlor, a pier, acres of board-and-batten cottages in neat rows, bathhouses, and a dance pavilion. In summer, it hosted a carnival complete with carousel, Ferris wheel, and other rides—and a sideshow featuring "geek" acts such as Snake Man and the Woman with No Body. During the war years, the Federal Works Agency built a bathhouse for the many Black servicemen stationed in the area, including the first Black marines at Montford Point. Buses ran from Fort Johnson and Camp Davis to a "Jim Crow loading zone" in Wilmington, where other buses carried the servicemen to Seabreeze. Gambling and moonshine liquor were readily available.

Now in the postwar boom, the Carolina Beach police still won't let Black visitors drive through that community to get to the ocean beaches of Seabreeze—separated from the soundside resort by the Intracoastal Waterway—so boats continue to ferry families across to the beaches.[7]

Besides the hotels, more than thirty juke joints offer dancing to the hottest numbers on a jukebox or piccolo. Some book live bands that play bebop, boogie, and swing music long into the night for the crowds of fashionably dressed dancers.

Segregation can keep Black and white audiences apart, but it can't contain the music. Two white brothers, Malcolm "Chicken"

Hicks and his brother Bobby, grew up going to dances in or near the Hayti district of Durham. At Skinny's, a shoeshine shop with a jukebox, they learned to dance to all the hot "race" records—bebop, boogie, and rhythm and blues—music with a 4/4 blues-shuffle beat that drives energetic dancing. By 1941, they were living in Carolina Beach. They got to know the vendors who stocked the jukebox records.[8]

Chicken recalls, "Then they'd be down servicing the jukebox, and one of them would say, 'Let's get the jug and go down to Seabreeze.' I'd go, okay, and we'd go down there and hear this music . . . the music at Seabreeze was different [from Carolina Beach] because it was black swing and black rhythm and blues where this [Carolina Beach] music was white."[9]

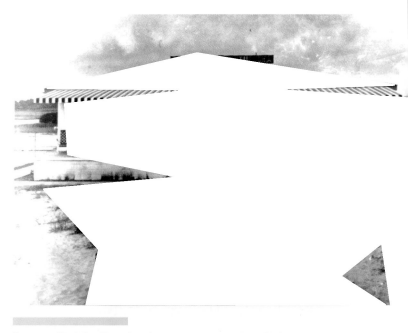

For many Black families, a beach vacation meant a trip to Seabreeze Resort and a stay at one of its hotels, such as Monte Carlo by the Sea.

Chicken persuades one jukebox owner to stock some Black records, and all of the sudden the music of Seabreeze is playing all over town. Teenaged white "Black dancers" filled up the joints.

One of the first is the Tijuana Inn operated by Jim Hannah, a former shipfitter and sometime bootlegger from Mecklenberg County, on the ground floor of the Ocean Plaza building on the boardwalk. It's such a draw that within two years he expands to a bowling alley across the street and christens it Bop City. More "jump joints" open along the strand, large enough for dancing crowds, and Beach Music takes hold—made up of rhythm and blues favorites like Amos Milburn's "Chicken Shack Boogie," Paul Williams's "The Huckle-Buck," and Count Basie's "One o'Clock Jump."

Seabreeze reaches its peak of popularity in the 1950s. Tourists can book into the Daley Hotel, the Hotel Faison, and the Breeze Inn. They can take their meals at the Edgewater Cafeteria or the Tavern, where they can also dance. A new hotel takes shape in 1951—Lulu Freeman Hill and her husband Frank relocate from Queens, New York, to a tract of land she owns in common with other heirs. They invest their life savings of $30,000 in building Monte Carlo by the Sea, the most ambitious resort hotel yet, a brilliant structure of whitewashed cement featuring a pavilion, bathhouse, and restaurant with wide dining porches shaded by striped awnings.[10]

Now the beachgoers come not only from inland counties but also from South Carolina and Virginia: social and business clubs, Boy and Girl Scouts, church groups. Seabreeze—also known as Freeman's Beach—attracts people from all walks of life. Assata Shakur (née JoAnne Byron), granddaughter of Frank and Lulu Freeman Hill, moves there as a child in 1950 with her parents. Her job is to stock the coolers with sodas, keep the potato chip racks full, and set the tables at Monte Carlo—and collect fifty cents per automobile at the entrance to the graded parking lot. She recalls in her memoir, "A lot of poor people came to the beach." Many are farm laborers from inland communities. "Sometimes the floors of their raggedy old cars or trucks were half rotted out. Usually a lot of little children were with them and they wouldn't have bathing suits. They went swimming in whatever clothes they had worn to the beach, and half the time the little kids wore nothing. Then there were those who came to put on airs, usually in the evening, all dressed up to eat dinner."

And the food was delectable. "Right now, when I think of the fried chicken and fish dinners, my mouth starts to water," Shakur remembers. "But what really sends me off is remembering those seafood platters with fish, shrimps, oysters, deviled crab, clam fritters, and French fries with lettuce and tomatoes on the side. If my memory is any good, I think they sold for $1.50."

Each restaurant offers its own specialty—fresh oysters and crabs harvested from the local sound, fried fish, and clam fritters fried in a batter of eggs, flour, onions, and other ingredients in secret recipes.

For many who come, Seabreeze is their first taste of the seashore. "One of the moving things for me was when someone saw the ocean for the first time," Shakur writes. "It was amazing to watch. They would stand there, in awe, overpowered and overwhelmed, as if they had come face to face with God or with the vastness of the universe."

And because of the lively music at all the juke joints and the open use of bootleg liquor, the resort attracts another kind of visitor. "Then there were the goodtimers," she writes. "Their cars smelled like whiskey. They would dance a lot, eat a lot, spend a lot on the piccolo, and many times I would wonder if they had made it home all right."[11]

Pulsing dance music is the heart of Seabreeze: Dinah Washington, Chuck Berry, Big Maybelle, Little Richard, and other hot performers blare from the jukeboxes, and players like Bo Diddley and Bobby "Blue" Bland keep the pavilions jumping with live music. Fats Domino and James Brown book in at the Loftin Hotel for gigs in Wilmington, where they are not permitted to stay in the segregated hotels.[12]

The hot beach music created by Black performers has jumped the race line, and its driving beat—heard now in Carolina Beach, Myrtle Beach, and other Carolina coastal towns—becomes the heartbeat of a new phenomenon the disc jockeys are calling "rock 'n' roll."

But midway through its heyday, disaster strikes Seabreeze. As the 1954 beach season comes to a close, on October 15, Hurricane Hazel slams ashore just southwest of Seabreeze, battering the resort with a twelve-foot storm surge and winds of up to 140 mph. All along the North Carolina coast, houses are washed away, buildings torn apart, streets and towns flooded, fleets of fishing boats wrecked in broken piles, even railroad locomotives washed off their tracks.[13]

At Seabreeze, the result is utter devastation—structures knocked down or washed away, the fishing pier reduced to a line of ragged pilings, the beach and sound side deeply eroded by the onslaught of water. Among the casualties is the Monte Carlo. "It had taken away everything," owner Frank Hill recalls. Few of the owners carry insurance, and those who try to rebuild have to contend with two more hurricanes the following season—Connie and Ione.[14]

Some owners, undaunted, rebuild their hotels and dance halls. But the old glory is gone. Seabreeze never quite recovers. The newly dredged Carolina Beach Inlet ruins the shellfishing grounds with sediment and causes massive erosion of the beach—more than a thousand feet of waterfront is lost.[15]

The music plays on at Seabreeze for another decade and a half, ever fainter, until at last it goes silent.[16]

As the sun sets over the Forest Drive-In, Glenn Miller's "Moonlight Serenade" played over the speakers, signaling the start of the movie. From 1949 until the theater closed in the mid-'70s, there was no finer way to spend a warm night in Raleigh.

CHAPTER

FAST FOOD AND **FLICKS**–THE DRIVE-IN CRAZE

The automobile becomes the signature vehicle of the decade—not the practical farm trucks and black sedans of the 1930s but long, sleek automobiles with wraparound windshields, fat whitewall tires, and jet-age tailfins—brightly painted in colors such as Chadron red, Vienna blue, and Safford cream.

The Carteret County *News-Times* advertises a Buick four-door sedan from Mobley Buick Co. in Morehead City with "de luxe finish, extra-wide seats" and "double bubble" taillights, riding on "low-pressure tires on wide, Safety-Ride rims, that stop heel-over and sway on curves" and gives you "freedom at last from jounce and jiggle": "You hardly know the road is there!"[1]

In the same issue, Lee Motor Sales, Inc., invites the public to "come meet the 1951 Kaiser . . . Tomorrow's car . . . Here Today!!"

And Parker Motors announces, "Now that our production lines are rolling again, we'll soon be able to show you the finest Chryslers and Plymouths in all our 25 years."[2]

No longer rationed to support the war effort and now in plentiful supply, gasoline costs about twenty cents per gallon.[3]

In 1950, the average family car costs between $1,500 and $2,200—some 30 to 50 percent more than the average annual income across the state, whose population numbers just over four million, and grows by almost half a million during the decade. More than a third of North Carolinians are now classified as "urban"—and that rises to 40 percent by the close of the decade.[4]

Racing stock cars on dirt tracks has been a popular, thrilling pastime in the western Piedmont since the 1930s, when bootleggers in souped-up whiskey cars staged informal Saturday afternoon races for bragging rights. Now the family car takes on a romance of its own, a marriage of speed and luxury. No longer is the automobile just a means of transportation—it becomes both a status symbol and a shared adventure. Being in the car, cruising the network of highways and country roads, is a pastime all to itself.

The new Eisenhower administration rolls out an ambitious plan for a national defense highway system to span the nation connecting East and West Coasts, the far North with the Deep South. Three of these new interstates—I-85, I-95, and I-40—advance into North Carolina. Soon drivers are speeding along more than five hundred miles of fast, four-lane freeways. Meanwhile, under an ambitious plan championed by Governor W. Kerr Scott ("Go Forward With Scott!"), the state builds twelve thousand miles of new farm-to-market roads and upgrades another fifteen thousand miles for all-weather travel. The new roads not only support farmers who need to transport their goods to warehouses and transshipment points; they also help stage another economic engine: the fourth biggest trucking industry in the country with more tractor trailers than any other state. Winston-Salem is home to the McLean Trucking Company, which advertises "the largest individually owned trucking terminal in the world."[5]

Following a national trend, drive-in restaurants pop up in cities and small towns, like Bar-B-Q King in West Charlotte and Short Sugar's Pit Bar-B-Q in Reidsville. Unlike the chains springing up across the country, the local places tend to serve homegrown favorites.

Drive-in movie theaters also cater to the new mobile patrons, such as the Moon-Glo Theatre in Henderson and the Sunset Drive-In in Shelby. Some of the movie theaters feature pickled eggs along with popcorn.

Families cruise the new interstates and freshly paved back roads in sleek, spruce green Buick sedans and Wedgewood blue Ford station wagons to park, feast, and enjoy the show, comfortably relaxed on plush, "sofa-wide" seats, without ever getting out of the car. The car itself becomes part of the entertainment.[6]

The first drive-in movie theater opened in Camden, New Jersey, in 1933—the brainchild of Richard Hollingshead, the general sales manager for his father's Whiz Auto Products Company, maker of greases, oils, and polishes. Hollingshead deliberately set out to invent a new cash business that would make his fortune. As he put it, he "analyzed the market from the standpoint of what people gave up last. It came out this way: Food. Clothing, Autos. Movies. In order." He determined that, even in hard times, Americans stubbornly attended the moving pictures.[7]

Hollingshead also investigated why some people didn't go to movies: "The mother says she's not dressed; the husband doesn't want to put on his shoes; the question is what to do with the kids; parking the car is difficult or maybe they have to pay for parking; even the seats in the theatre may not be comfortable to contemplate."[8]

Like earlier entrepreneurs who came up with the idea of showing moving pictures at indoor theaters designed especially for movies—rather than at makeshift venues—he hit upon the notion of an open-air theater designed for an audience in their cars. He experimented with the idea in his own backyard by projecting movies from his 1928 Kodak, mounted on the hood of his car, onto a screen nailed to a tree. Then he tried out the view from cars parked in various places on his driveway, simulating bad weather with a lawn sprinkler, even hitting on the need to raise the front wheels of cars so each provided a windshield view

Speakers at the drive-in allowed moviegoers to enjoy the sounds of the movies from the comfort of their cars.

of the screen. The "Drive-In Theatre" at Camden projected sound through an RCA "directional sound" system of three speakers and charged "25c Per Car and for Each Person 25c," or a family admission for $1.[9]

Only a handful of such open-air theaters—known as "ozoners"—operated throughout the 1930s. But the idea catches on with the automobile boom of the 1950s, when more than four thousand drive-ins around the country provide family entertainment on big screens, with sound now crackling out of speakers attached to the car doors and refreshments available at the central concession stand or from roving snack carts. In August 1952 alone, across the country 40.9 million paying patrons attend outdoor movies—over a million more than attend indoor theaters—and this doesn't count children under twelve, who typically are allowed in free to encourage attendance by the core audience—families. In 1948, North Carolina supports just sixty-six ozoners. By 1958, it has more than two hundred.[10]

The Moon-Glo premieres in July 1949 with *Ali Baba and the Forty Thieves*—starring Maria Montez, christened the "Caribbean Cyclone" for her exotic, sexy portrayals of damsels in distress, and Jon Hall, a handsome B-movie actor known for his star turns in such memorable flicks as *The Lion Man* and *The Invisible Man's Revenge*—playing along with three cartoons.[11]

Parents no longer have to pay for babysitters to enjoy a night out—the whole family can be bundled into the car and taken along, then fed relatively cheaply. Indeed, *America's Baby Book* advises, "If you have a car, baby can sleep in the back seat while both parents enjoy the movie at a drive-in theater."[12]

At the drive-in movie theater, patrons sit out under the stars in a field of automobiles and enjoy their dinner out.

Because the movies are shown outdoors, where any passerby can see them, theaters often book a double feature. The first half of the bill typically is a wholesome title that can be viewed by children as well as adults. Then, during a long intermission, viewers are encouraged by onscreen trailers to visit the concession stand. The second, more adult feature plays later in the evening when the youngest kids have fallen asleep. A poll of drive-in owners finds that the most popular films are Westerns, closely followed by action films, comedies, and musicals. The open-air movies are especially popular in rural areas, where land is cheap and abundant and indoor theaters are scarce. Polling shows that the drive-ins are most popular with working-class people—not white-collar professionals. And many patrons cite the health benefits of being outdoors in fresh air and keeping their children safe from infectious diseases like flu or measles, which can be passed in crowded indoor spaces.[13]

Small drive-ins provide parking for as few as fifty cars, but the largest can accommodate two or even three thousand. Some feature playgrounds, horseshoe pits, and miniature golf courses—to encourage families to arrive long before showtime and spend more money at the concession stand, where a box of plain popcorn typically costs just ten cents—twenty cents with butter. One phenomenon that the state doesn't have is a "Fly-in Drive-in Theater" like the one in Asbury Park, New Jersey, which sets aside parking spaces for twenty-five airplanes. They land nearby and taxi to spaces in the rear row.[14]

The ozoners in North Carolina run the gamut. In Rockingham County, the Eden Drive-In advertises a capacity of two hundred cars. The Twilite, in Nakina, in Columbus County just north of the South Carolina border, holds just sixty.[15]

Albemarle offers the Badin Road; Hickory the Thunderbird; Raleigh the Tower and Forest Drive-Ins; and Bessemer City the Kings Mountain Drive-In.[16]

In Durham, the concession stand at the three-hundred-car Starlite Drive-In peddles—in addition to the usual popcorn—bug repellant coils, pickles, eggs, and hot sausage.[17]

The Forest Drive-In hosted bingo and pig races and even had a merry-go-round, but it was best known for showing feature films suitable for the whole family. At intermission, moviegoers could get popcorn and a Pepsi to enjoy on the hoods of their cars.

At the Park Drive-In in Greensboro, patrons can order through the audio speaker from a menu provided at the gate and have the food delivered right to their car. On a good night, a drive-in can make up to 40 percent of its box office gross from food concessions.[18]

Wilmington is home to at least four drive-ins: the Starway and the Skyline, on Carolina Beach Road; the North 17 drive-in; and the Wrightsville Road Drive-In. Jessiebeth Brady Geddie remembers date nights at the Wrightsville with her future husband, John, in his sleek white Plymouth Savoy with rocket tail fins. "You had to hook the speakers on the side window, and we had a little coil that lit would keep mosquitoes from eating you alive," she recalls. "Usually you carried popcorn and bottles of Coke with you."[19]

After the movie, the high school gang gathers at Mil-Jo, a nearby drive-in restaurant owned by Mildred and Joseph Hines. Mil-Jo's lot is itself as big as a small drive-in movie theater—holding more than sixty cars. Cruising couples can park under a wide canopy and order pizza burgers, crab burgers, and fifteen-cent hot dogs through a two-way radio mounted on a stanchion, then wait for the carhop to deliver the food right to the car. A disc jockey from WMFD 630 AM spins platters in a glass booth outside the restaurant, broadcasting nightly. The place is so popular that it backs up traffic and on weekend nights is patrolled by off-duty police officers. Highway patrolmen sometimes wait in ambush nearby to catch hot-rodding kids.[20]

The Mil-Jo is just one of the many drive-in restaurants opening up around the state. National chains are just getting started—McDonald's (a former barbecue joint now specializing in the fifteen-cent hamburger) in San Bernardino, California; Insta-Burger King in Jacksonville, Florida; Taco Bell in Downey, California; and Top Hat—later Sonic—in Shawnee, Oklahoma.

North Carolina drive-ins often feature more southern fare, tied to its long tradition of pulled-pork barbecue. Or, more righty, *traditions*—vinegary sauce in the east and sweet-spicy Lexington style in the Piedmont. Local barbecue joints take pride in their own closely held recipes for dry rubs and sauces. Short Sugar's Pit Bar-B-Q in Reidsville, northeast of Winston Salem, offers hand-pulled pork barbecue in sauce, as well as a wide breakfast-to-dinner menu that includes fried eggs, hot dogs, sandwiches, and platters. Diners pull up outside and eat in their cars, or else perch on the swivel-stools at the inside counter, visible through the floor-to-ceiling plateglass windows. Customers spot it from Scales Street by the rectangular white column towering above the low-slung building, emblazoned with the name in vertical letters.

The name is attributed to Eldridge Overby, who with his brothers, Johnny and Clyde, built Overby Brothers Drive-In. Eldridge wasn't a tall man, and the story goes that his girlfriend called him to dance with her to her favorite jukebox tune by saying, "I want to dance with my short sugar." Eldridge dies in a car crash before opening day, so his brothers name the place in his honor.[21]

In West Charlotte, the Bar-B-Q King—with its red and blue neon sign declaring "curb service"—doesn't get going until 1959, but it, too, quickly gains a loyal clientele on busy Wilkinson Boulevard, the fast route to the airport. Pork and chicken barbecue in thick tangy sauce are the stars of the menu, but customers can also order burgers, hot dogs, or fried seafood, served on a tray that rolls up to the car door.[22]

The drive-in culture is about more than convenience—it's a wholly American adventure, conceived in mobility and dedicated to casual comfort, all under the restless driver's control. Gone is the formality of the dining room table—or even the restaurant booth. The sideboard is hitched onto the driver's door, and plates sit in the lap.

As the decade turns to 1960, McDonald's opens its first restaurant in the state in Greensboro. Wilbur Hardee, an experienced restaurateur from Greenville, checks it out—even photographs it—and decides he can do better. He picks out a site on 14th Street not far from East Carolina University, then builds a smaller version of a McDonald's red-and-white tiled store, its two service windows shaded by a canted overhang supported by twin H-shaped pillars. The menu is spare: burgers (fifteen cents plain, twenty cents with cheese), French fries, apple pie, soft drinks, and milkshakes. "Best menu I ever had," Hardee later recalls in an interview. Hardee's is an overnight hit—the first of what becomes a chain of burger restaurants eventually featuring another Carolina favorite, homemade buttermilk biscuits and gravy.[23]

An old farmstead tradition of eating outside now takes place on the comfort of upholstered seats. And the automobile satisfies the restless craving to be in motion—even when it is parked.

Finch's Drive-In opened on Peace Street in Raleigh in the 1940s. The burgers, milkshakes, and "chicken boxes"—served curbside— proved so popular that the drive-in soon became a cafeteria.

In the 1950s, passengers wearing their fashionable best—coats and ties for men, dresses or suits for women—crossed the Cape Fear River on Atlantic Coast Line (ACL) trains that connected Wilmington to Rocky Mount and Florence, South Carolina. The railroad's busy riverfront station was a familiar presence in downtown Wilmington.

CHAPTER

LAST TRAIN OUT

A s fleets of family automobiles jam the new highways and passengers eagerly take to the air aboard Piedmont Airlines and other carriers, the era of mass rail travel is coming to an end—though in 1950, that seems unthinkable to the millions for whom railroads have always been ubiquitous and reliable. Rail travel has long enjoyed an aura of romance and adventure, steeped in history and imposing physical presence—a network of rights-of-way, trestles, and tunnels carved into the land itself. During the war, railroad platforms were the stages for millions of dramatic leave-takings and homecomings. No automobile horn or jet engine can stir the deep thrill of longing carried by the sound of a far-off train whistle in the night.

Yet while freight-carrying remains highly profitable, passenger service requires an ever-increasing investment: more and better seating; dining and sleeping facilities; large stations with amenities; and wages for both train crews and hospitality staff.

And federal regulations require carriers to provide service in the public interest to remote locations, where paying ridership is thin. Wartime travel during the first half of the 1940s provided a wild surge in demand—ninety-five billion passenger miles in the peak year of 1944 alone, more than four times as many as before the war. But now demand is receding to prewar levels—and being eroded further by energetic competition.

At the 1953 meeting of the National Association of Railroad and Utilities Commissioners (NARUC), the "special passenger deficit problem committee" reports that the loss of passenger traffic has escalated "from a problem to a serious threat to the economic stability of the railroads," concluding, "it's going to be difficult to convince railroad management of the wisdom of voluntarily investing more of their rapidly vanishing capital funds into better passenger equipment in the face of today's un-favorable prospects of gaining any return on such investment."[1]

By the mid-1950s, the airlines have siphoned off many first-class travelers, and automobiles have reduced coach travelers by a third. What seems to the rail traveler like a prosperous enterprise is, in fact, one that is struggling to break even.[2]

Railroads have been the arteries of the state and nation since before the Civil War, reaching from the coastal plain deep into the mountain west, knitting together cities and states on every point of the compass. In 1840, the Wilmington & Raleigh line (later Wilmington & Weldon, or W & W) in North Carolina was the longest continuous stretch of track in the world, 161.5 miles. During the Civil War, it became an iron lifeline to Confeder-ate troops in Virginia, hauling foodstuffs, troops, and matériel north from the blockade-runners' port of Wilmington until the capture of Fort Fisher in 1865.

Since 1900, the W & W has been incorporated into the Atlan-tic Coast Line Railroad (ACL), whose busy system of rails serves the Eastern Seaboard from Richmond to South Florida and inland as far as Birmingham, Alabama, as well as connecting with westbound routes. It is famous for its fast New York–to–Miami trains, christened with colorful names: *Vacationer, Florida Special, Everglades, Palmetto, Miamian, Florida Arrow, Gulf Coast Limited,* and *Havana Special. Champion,* originated in 1939 to compete with the Seaboard Air Line's *Silver Meteor* and named for the president of the line, Champion McDowell Davis, even inspires a song by Jack Rollins, who co-wrote "Frosty the Snowman" for Gene Autry.[3]

Like its predecessor, the Wilmington & Weldon, ACL is headquartered in Wilmington, in 1950 a fast-growing city of about 45,000. Some 1,500 local men and women work for ACL, which occupies an extensive complex of offices, maintenance sheds, machine shops, switching yards, and a massive roundhouse with a turntable for rotating engines onto a spiderweb of tracks, as well as a station and long platform sheds. Their presence near the riverfront keeps the downtown busy, and the ACL injects an annual payroll of $6.5 million into the city's economy.[4]

Wilmington lies between Richmond, Virginia, and Jacksonville, the line's busy Florida hub. But the city is also far east of the main line, located on the jutting coastal elbow of the state.

Trains make up in New York and travel to Washington, D.C., hauled by locomotives from a rival line such as the Pennsylvania Railroad; they continue from D.C. to Richmond via the Richmond, Fredericksburg & Potomac Railroad; then they change to ACL engines to run on ACL-owned track. But the through-trains don't come to Wilmington—instead, they cut straight across from Wilson to Florence, South Carolina, then continue south. Wilmington is the end of the line—each day, one or two passenger cars are shunted to Wilson or Rocky Mount to be coupled to trains like *Vacationer* or *Champion.* Just one or two local trains a day serve the city.

In 1939, ACL began its program of "dieselization"—updating its fleet of steam locomotives to diesel units—but the war slowed the transition. During the war years, every locomotive was pressed into service, ferrying troops and hauling matériel, as well as carrying civilian passengers for business and pleasure. But by 1955, most of ACL's black steam locomotives have been sent to the Emerson "boneyard" in Rocky Mount, where salvagers cut apart the great machines for their scrap value.

The new locomotives are bullet-nosed, streamlined E-series diesels, built by GM's Electro Motive Division and painted with stylish royal purple livery accented by a broad silver side-stripe trimmed in yellow—a color scheme chosen personally by Champ Davis.

The sleek, modern engines and flashy paint jobs are designed to catch the traveler's eye and show rail travel to be modern and up-to-date. Automobile touring is fast becoming the new trend for middle-class vacationers, and regional airlines such as Piedmont are now connecting travelers to distant cities in record time. Airlines, airports, and highways are receiving hefty government subsidies. Still, the old-fashioned luxury of the passenger train remains appealing for many, especially on the Florida route. Riders can board in New York and step off the train in Miami twenty-four hours later. They can make the journey in the privacy of their own roomette or choose a Pullman sleeping berth instead. And even if they travel in the day coach, the seats are broad, plush, and roomy enough for comfort.

And trains are safer than either cars or airplanes: in 1951, passenger deaths per million miles traveled due to rail mishaps are one third those of airlines. Pullman, the maker of sleeper cars, reinforces this point in an ad featuring a traveler waving goodbye to his wife and kids from the window of a train. "I have three good reasons for going Pullman," reads the text, then drives home the not-so-subtle message in all caps: "COMFORTABLE,

DEPENDABLE, AND—ABOVE ALL—SAFE." The ad inspires an outraged response in *Aviation Week*, which calls it "Pullman's Vicious Ad."[5]

But the constant and massive traffic engendered by the war has worn out ACL's track, stations, and rolling stock, as it has for many other American railroads. Upgrading worn-out track is not just about providing more comfortable passage—it's an urgent matter of safety.

On the bitterly cold winter night of December 16, 1943, a single faulty rail set off a calamitous chain of events. The southbound *Tamiami West Coast Champion*, enroute with eighteen cars from New York to St. Petersburg and running more than an hour late, was passing near Rennert in Robeson County when it crossed a split rail at eighty-five miles per hour. Two Pullman sleepers and the dining car jumped the tracks—and came to rest partially blocking the northbound tracks. The fireman sent to flag down oncoming northbound trains slipped on the frozen snow and disabled his warning flare.

Frank Belknap, the engineer of the northbound *Tamiami East Coast Champion*, speeding north at eighty miles per hour and loaded with servicemen bound home for the holidays, was unaware of the blocked track ahead. Belknap had forty-five years of experience, but by the time the obstruction was visible, there was little he could do to stop a quarter mile of speeding steel. In the last moments, he was blinded by the glaring headlamp of the stalled southbound locomotive. The northbound *Champion* slammed into the derailed train with explosive impact. Eight of its sixteen cars jumped the track, and three telescoped into one another with catastrophic effect. Bodies were hurled through the air and crushed inside the twisted steel carriages, many dismembered and mutilated beyond recognition. Seventy-two passengers died—fifty-two of them servicemen—and 187 other passengers and crew were injured, making it the deadliest railway crash in North Carolina history.

A split rail was again the culprit in the wreck of the Waycross, Georgia, to Montgomery, Alabama, train just before midnight on August 4, 1944, at Stockton, Georgia. Five cars—including a Red Cross hospital car carrying wounded soldiers from the Normandy battlefield—derailed and smashed into a freight train stopped on a siding to let the through-train pass. Car number ten was peeled open all along its side by the sixty-five-mile-per-hour impact. The death toll was forty-seven—many of them members of a Black railway work gang heading home. Volunteer rescue workers flailed about in the dark until truckloads of soldiers arrived from nearby Moody Field. They set up searchlights and illuminated the scene, and the grisly rescue effort went on through daylight.

In its investigative report, the Interstate Commerce Commission noted that more than sixty accidents had been caused by defective rails since 1939, most of them, fortunately, nonfatal.[6]

With the war years behind, ACL president Champion McDowell Davis begins a comprehensive program to upgrade its rails and other infrastructure and replace aging passenger cars—for now, defying the daunting odds of turning a profit. The ACL suffers no more fatal wrecks throughout the 1950s.

Through his own long career, Davis epitomizes the rise of railroads from a chancy beginning to a preeminent position in America's culture and economy. The son of a timer for the Wilmington & Weldon, he started as a messenger boy in 1893 at the age of thirteen and by 1942 was running the "standard railroad of the South." He is tall and self-assured, dresses in smart suits with old-fashioned stiff-collared shirts, and is famous for his colorful profanity—a boss who demands perfection.

Tall, self-assured, and with a penchant for colorful profanity, Champion McDowell Davis was known for being a boss who demanded perfection.

Davis runs the line from his rolling office car, touring stations during weekdays and home in time for the weekly Sunday morning staff meeting. His all-male secretarial staff during the war years includes Claude Howell, a photographer and painter who often depicts workingmen at their jobs—stylized figures of stevedores and fishermen rendered in seacoast pastels or bright, vivid colors. As an ACL employee, he takes advantage of discounted tickets to travel to New York and elsewhere for summer study with premier artists.[7]

Among the innovations Davis has introduced are centralized traffic controls; reflective paint on station signs, mileposts, and car ID numbers; and on the improved double-tracked mainline, a breathtaking speed limit of ninety miles per hour for passenger trains.

Champ Davis has prospered by adapting to the times, and so must ACL. The tremendous pressures of catering to the needs of all those trainloads of servicemen and women has made the railroad staff expert at logistics: storing and preparing food, feeding passengers in continuous shifts, efficiently managing sleeping arrangements, sorting and stowing luggage. Now they put that expertise to good use.

Airlines are adding in-flight pursers and stewardesses, so ACL hires its own hostesses to wait on passengers. Dining cars become more elegant, featuring linen tablecloths, bone china, silverware, and silver tea services. In-season fresh local fruits and vegetables replace canned foods whenever possible. Menus offer more variety, including many upscale choices.

The *Palmetto Limited*, for example, features a full dinner menu, including Florida grapefruit, Carolina sweet potatoes glacé, chicken gumbo Creole, fillet of fresh-caught fish sauté meunière, assorted bread, and pumpkin custard pie—a whole meal for $1.50, complemented by claret or sauterne at forty cents per glass (domestic) or sixty cents (imported).[8]

The aura of leisurely elegance is enhanced by celebrities—in 1951, the abdicated Edward, Duke of Windsor, and his wife, Wallis (Simpson) Windsor, sign an ACL menu card, endorsing the claim that the line is fit for royalty.[9]

Because it is impractical to attach more than one dining car per train, racial segregation is achieved by means of stylish partitions made of etched glass that separate white diners from "colored." Likewise, engineers, conductors, and hostesses are white, while firemen, cooks, servers, and porters are Black. Like airports, train stations maintain separate "white" and "colored" waiting rooms, drinking fountains, and restrooms.

Travelers usually wear their best—suits and ties for men, floral-print dresses or suits for women.

To pass the time, ACL offers movies, games, and music in the club car—along with special entertainments. "All aboard the 'Florida Special' for SUN 'N' FUN FASHIONS!" reads a broadside in the *ACL News* for March–April 1959. It advertises in-ride fashion shows in the club car, featuring swimsuit models showing off the latest beachwear.

But across the country, passenger revenues have still been declining steeply. Railroad executives petition the federal government to allow them to jettison unprofitable passenger routes. Partly this is to allow them to concentrate their efforts and resources on freight service, which remains profitable—though it, too, has slipped. The Transportation Act of 1958 allows them to do just that, if the service is not "required by public convenience and necessity." Never again will passenger rail service be as widespread and familiar as it has been for the first half of the twentieth century.

In Wilmington, the shifting economy of rail service takes an ominous turn. Against the opposition of Champ Davis, the board of the ACL decides to relocate its headquarters to Jacksonville, Florida. They announce the move on December 10,

1955—known forever after as Black Thursday—but it awaits the construction of a towering new office building.

When the new headquarters building is complete in July 1960, the ACL packs some nine hundred families aboard special trains bound for Jacksonville, complete with boxcars full of their household belongings and flatcars full of their automobiles. The red-brick complex of roundhouse, sheds, shops, and offices is mostly demolished—the land deeded to the city for construction of a junior college: Cape Fear Technical Institute. One of its trustees is a familiar figure, now retired from the railroad: Champion McDowell Davis.

The station remains a little longer—until 1968, when the last passenger train pulls out of Wilmington, and a way of life disappears down the tracks.[10]

By the 1950s, the ACL roundhouse in downtown Wilmington illustrated the evolution of the locomotive, from No. 250, a Baldwin steam engine built in 1910, to the diesel-powered No. 427, circa 1950.

From the beginning, the founders of WUNC-TV made it a mission to provide programming for the whole family, including a production of Snow White in July 1958.

CHAPTER

UNC ON
THE AIR

Public Television in North Carolina begins as a quiet, static signal: invisible, very high frequency (VHF) waves, emanating from a broadcast tower nearly eight hundred feet tall on Terrell's Mountain in Chatham County, create a test pattern on television sets in a radius of a hundred miles. The test pattern appears on Channel 4 from noon until 6:30 pm for several days in January 1955, and residents of cities as far away as Statesville call or send postcards to the Consolidated University of North Carolina office to let Robert F. Schenkkan, director of the newly created WUNC-TV, know that viewers are receiving the signal clearly. Indeed, the signal has been picked up as far west as Kansas and Missouri.[1]

The university has for the past decade sought to extend its educational mission across the entire state through the establishment of campuses and centers. Now it takes that mission to the airwaves, connecting households in the Piedmont region to UNC through educational, cultural, and college sports programming. No longer will citizens have to be physically present on campus to benefit from the well of knowledge and expertise gathered there.

In the same way that the rural electrification program of the 1930s, '40s, and early '50s lit up the hinterland and made possible a radio net that spread news and popular music throughout the state, the educational TV station will create a net of learning, reaching into far-flung households, bringing at least some important assets of the university to any citizen who wants to be included.

The inaugural broadcast of January 8, 1955, opens with a film (a Donald O'Connor–Susanna Foster romantic comedy called *This Is the Life*), followed by a live half-hour song and dance program.

The evening lineup features a basketball doubleheader between Wake Forest University and the University of North Carolina at Chapel Hill. To position the two bulky cameras for an optimum high-angle view of the action in Woolen Gymnasium, the production crew sledgehammers an opening in the second-story cinder block wall. Local radio stations, wary of competition, prevail upon WUNC-TV to broadcast only the black-and-white video—"broadvision"—not audio. Thus the first sports show is a silent moving picture. Carolina wins 95–78—a good omen for this new enterprise, only the tenth educational TV station in the country. As the tenth, it qualifies for the last $10,000 educational grant from the Emerson Radio and Phonograph Corporation.[2]

It's fitting that the first big evening show should be a sporting contest—William C. Friday, assistant to UNC President Gordon Gray and one of the main architects of WUNC-TV, served as sports editor of NC State's campus newspaper, the *Technician*. He also spent many autumn afternoons while an undergraduate working as a "spotter" for the broadcast announcer at football games.[3]

Equally fitting is the first night's sign-off program: Edward R. Murrow's "This I Believe." Murrow introduced the program in 1951 with these words: "This I Believe. By that name, we present the personal philosophies of thoughtful men and women in all walks of life. In this brief space, a banker or a butcher, a painter or a social worker, people of all kinds who need have nothing

As one of the founding fathers of WUNC-TV, William C. Friday envisioned the station as an educational opportunity for viewers across the state.

more in common than integrity, a real honesty, will write about the rules they live by, the things they have found to be the basic values in their lives." Friday is himself a man of deep convictions, integrity, and honesty—a believer in the power of higher education to make North Carolina a better place.[4]

Programming for Channel 4 originates from one of three studios, each affiliated with a campus of the Consolidated University: a renovated laundry in Greensboro, a converted dining hall in Chapel Hill, and a newly constructed studio in Raleigh. A retrofitted Trailways bus—donated for the purpose—serves as a mobile studio. From the start, the vision for WUNC-TV is to send its cameras and crew wherever the stories are.[5]

The whole venture is born in 1952 when the Federal Communications Commission (FCC) makes available eight channels in the state for use by noncommercial stations. President Gray calls together a meeting of directors and deans from the three campuses—Chapel Hill, Raleigh, and Greensboro—and gets the green light from the Board of Trustees by the following year.[6]

But there's a hitch—one that almost sinks the enterprise before it can even launch: Joseph Bryan, president of Jefferson Standard Broadcasting, which operates WBTV Channel 3 Charlotte, also wants Channel 4 to get better media penetration in the important Triangle market. But when he finds out UNC wants the channel, he generously withdraws his bid—and more than that, supplies the university with all the completed paperwork relevant to the application, a gift worth thousands of dollars that would otherwise have been spent on legal and other fees.[7]

Behind the scenes, Friday works with two other men to make the television venture possible: William Donald "Billy" Carmichael Jr., chief finance officer for UNC; and big band leader James Kern "Kay" Kyser, a Rocky Mount native and UNC alum.

Kyser first led a dance band in 1926 while still a student and member of the cheerleading squad. So ardent was his school spirit that he wrote the fight song, "Tar Heels on Hand." He took the band on tour, playing theaters, dances, and clubs, landing a weekly musical comedy quiz program broadcast nationally on NBC radio: *Kay Kyser's Kollege of Musical Knowledge*, which ran for more than a decade.

When war broke out, Kyser vowed to play no more commercial gigs until victory, choosing instead to entertain the troops and make morale-boosting movies. He performed overseas on far-flung Pacific islands, starred in movies such as *Carolina Blues*, and, later, a television reprise of Kay Kyser's Kollege of Musical Knowledge on NBC-TV.

In 1951—after scoring thirty-five top-ten records and eleven Number 1 hits—he retires from show business and settles in Chapel Hill. There he and his wife, Georgia—once a singer in his band—became close friends with Bill and Ida Friday, sharing dinners and ideas.[8]

With the strong support of President Gray, Friday, Carmichael, and Kyser develop a vision for an educational TV station that will extend the reach of the university and serve all the people who support it through their taxes. Friday acts according to a deeply ingrained progressive ethic: the university should foster socially responsible civic leadership. To do that, it needs to connect not just to students but also to the larger public. And broadcast television is an effective way to make that connection.[9]

For three years, Kyser, Friday, and Carmichael embark on a different kind of tour, crisscrossing the state in search of dollars to fund the new venture. In this fashion, they raise $1.8 million in cash and services from more than twenty companies, leveraged against a modest initial appropriation of $217,000 from the legislature.[10]

From the outset, WUNC-TV leaders set lofty goals for the enterprise. In 1955, the director, Robert Schenkkan, tells his colleagues at a meeting of the American College Public Relations Association, "We must create a programming policy which has sufficient variety and breadth of appeal, so that the educational station is vital as well as educational."[11]

In 1956, the station itself becomes a classroom for students—not just from UNC, but also from Meredith, NC State, Peace, and St. Mary's—who help achieve that vitality.

That spring, the student producers at WUNC-TV receive national attention for the first television adaptation of William Saroyan's *Hello Out There*—a short play set in a small Texas town in which a young itinerant gambler is jailed on a false charge of rape, falls in love with the jailhouse cook with whom he plots escape, but instead is set upon by a lynch mob led by the purported victim's husband. It's an ambitious project, exactly the kind of program that fulfills the mission of educating by entertaining.[12]

At the Raleigh studios, Roy Johnston and his professional crew offer students workshops in the elements of broadcast production: operating a camera, setting up lights, staging scenery, directing actors and other on-screen personalities, and operating the control board.

"Every Tuesday and Thursday afternoons, nine Meredith girls will be seen in Bermuda shorts or blue jeans leaving for WUNC-TV," reports the Meredith College *Twig* on March 16. "Upon reaching the studio one might see Joyce Herndon frantically pushing the numerous switches in the control room, or Kitty Holt with her earphones trying to tell Liz Jones to get Camera One in focus on Margaret Tucker and at the same time listening to Jean Puckett who is working with the lights. In another section of the studio Janice Dennis might be seen turning pale because Nancy Young has assembled the wrong scenery, or because Mary Edna Grimes has Camera Two focused on the ceiling instead of Kay McCosley."

Viewers across North Carolina could learn about history with Lois Ettinger and about the landscape of their state on *Variety Vacationland*.

At the end of their apprenticeship, all the young women from Meredith participate in a series of televised dramas.[13]

Some courses of study are offered via broadcast. Fifteen managers and foremen of the Automatic Blanket plant in Smithfield complete a class in supervisory and management development, offered in ten televised installments.[14]

After President Gray resigns to accept a position in the Eisenhower administration, Friday is appointed interim president of UNC in 1956 at the age of thirty-five, and within a year, the appointment becomes permanent. He remains president for thirty years—making him the longest-serving university president of the twentieth century—always a tireless supporter of public television. One of his goals is to extend the broadcast reach of WUNC-TV to all one hundred counties. Within five years, he makes significant progress: four more stations are approved, and the invisible VHF signal can now reach 60 percent of the state.[15]

By 1960, the WUNC-TV schedule features a wide-ranging lineup of informative programs. It offers music: *Two Centuries of Symphony*, *Serenade*, and *Spotlight on Opera*. Education: *Trigonometry*, *Geology 41: The College Year*, and *Understanding School Music Literature*. Public service: *Social Security in Action* and *Today on the Farm*. Even history and geopolitics: *Yesterday's Worlds* and *Commonwealth of Nations*. And news at midday, evening, and night.[16]

Friday's behind-the-scenes role transforms into an on-camera presence in 1970, when the station debuts *North Carolina People*—a one-on-one interview show that takes full advantage of his warmth, frankness, encyclopedic knowledge of the state, and his talent for putting his guests at ease. Playwright Paul Green, novelist Doris Betts, journalist David Brinkley, and other leaders in culture, the arts, politics, business, and education take their turns in the guest chair—along with every living governor.

"Uncle Billy," as he is known to the students and staff at the station, projects a quiet sense of trust leavened with gentle humor. The show gains a large and faithful following and airs for more than four decades, making it the longest-running program in the history of WUNC-TV—which does, at last, fulfill his vision and reach into all one hundred counties.[17]

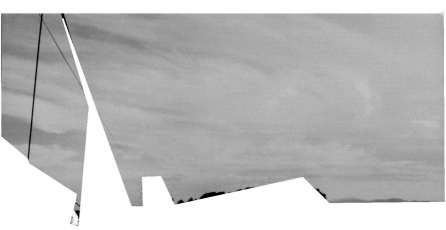

After photographer Hugh Morton inherited Grandfather Mountain, he built the Mile-High Swinging Bridge on Linville Peak—now an iconic part of our mountain landscape.

CHAPTER

A MAN AND HIS MOUNTAIN

When Hugh MacRae Morton inherits Grandfather Mountain in 1952, he understands that the 4,500-acre tract is a spectacular legacy—more than a mountain cresting at Calloway Peak, more than near-vertical stands of spruce and hardwoods that have somehow survived the aggressive logging of his grandfather's day, more than just real estate to be developed into homes and commercial enterprises. It is a treasure to be valued and preserved for posterity. He's been a well-known professional photographer for more than a decade, and he sees the familiar landscape with a photographer's eye for natural beauty.[1]

He does develop it in a specific way: to make it more accessible to visitors, to highlight the magisterial view from Linville Peak, and to ensure that the vast acreage surrounding the access road remains unspoiled—a wild haven for animals, a sanctuary for trees and plants. He becomes both an entrepreneur in the booming tourism trade and the guardian of the mountain.[2]

He turns the single-lane toll road constructed over the original horse trail by his grandfather, Hugh MacRae—president of the Linville Improvement Company—into a two-lane graded road. Formerly, the road stopped about two-thirds of the way up the mountain. Travelers tethered their horses or parked their automobiles at an overlook called Observation Point (later called Cliffside)—from where, on a clear day, they could see the skyline of Charlotte eighty miles away to the southeast—then hiked the steep, rocky trail to the top.[3]

Morton extends the graded road to a parking area between Linville Peak and another, called simply Second Peak. And if arriving at that 5,946-foot-high summit of the most rugged mountain in the Southeast is not enough to lure drivers up the steep, curving track, he erects a modern marvel on Linville Peak itself: the Mile-High Swinging Bridge, so named because it stands at 5,305 feet above sea level.[4] The 228-foot-long bridge spans a chasm eighty feet deep. The wooden deck of the bridge is suspended on cables between two steel towers. Between each of the deck planks is a joint, so when the wind blows—and it nearly always blows at this altitude—the bridge swings. It is anchored by stout steel cables bolted into the rock, spring-loaded with great coils to absorb the shock of the wind load—gusts of over one hundred miles per hour are not uncommon. The bridge is prefabricated in Greensboro by the Truitt Manufacturing Company and reassembled on site in three weeks. Gubernatorial candidate William B. Umstead dedicates it, and his nine-year-old daughter, Merle, is the first person to walk across it.[5]

It is said that the Cherokee called the mountain *Tanawha*—after the "fabulous hawk" that nested there—and early settlers discerned in its craggy profile the face of a recumbent old man staring at the sky—in fact, several profiles from several vantage points—and called it Grandfather Mountain.[6]

It rises four thousand feet out of the high Piedmont Plain, part of the "Grandfather Window," a pre-Cambrian sheet of solid rock forced up and over younger rock in the violent collision of the African and North American tectonic plates some 300 million years ago, so that stratigraphy—the marker of geologic time formed by the layers of rock—is inverted. Giant boulders such as Split Rocks and Sphinx—the latter of which weighs in at 2 million pounds—had already formed in ancient streambeds some 640 million years ago and were thrust into the air by the force of the upheaval. Millions of years ago, Grandfather Mountain may have been as high as the Alps, but erosion has worn it down to its present height of 5,946 feet.[7]

Grandfather Mountain is more than just a peak or even a series of peaks. It's a spectacular, wild ecological island in the Blue Ridge Mountains. They, in turn, form part of a chain of Appalachians stretching more than 600 miles from Pennsylvania to Georgia. Ten miles long and about three miles wide, Grandfather encompasses 150 square miles or 100,000 acres. Visitors climb through 16 different habitats—defined by topography, weather, forest cover, and—above all—altitude. On a spring morning when the temperature at the base is in the 70s, a thermometer at the summit might record 50—the temperature of Newfoundland. In summer the temperature at the peak might rise as high as the 80s, and in winter it can dip into the negative 30s.[8]

Black bears with coats ranging from jet-black to cinnamon roam the slopes and canyons, and cougars hunt the twilit paths. Elk were once plentiful, until they were hunted out in the eighteenth century. Now, only deer can be spotted furtively browsing. All told, more than seventy rare or endangered species inhabit Grandfather Mountain, including twenty-one different species of salamander, with colorful names like Weller, Yohnalossee, Northern shovel-nosed, pigmy, and the two–and-a-half-pound hellbender—which tips the scale at three pounds and is the second largest salamander species in the world.[9]

Both the Linville and Wautauga rivers, flowing east and west respectively, spring from Grandfather, as does a slew of creeks, including Little Wilson, Wilson, Slackwater, and Upper Boone Fork. The creeks teem with native brook trout and freshwater mussels and are also home to river otters, beaver, and mink. The woods and underbrush shelter gray and red fox, long-tailed weasels, cottontails, snowshoe hares, two varieties of skunks (the Eastern-striped or "polecat" and the spotted or civet cat), and the two-inch-long pygmy shrew—the smallest known mammal in North America.

More than a hundred species of breeding birds populate the cliffs, forest, and balds, including twenty species of warblers. At least five species of owls hunt the forest and clearings, as does the black-hooded peregrine falcon, with a wingspan of more than three feet. The canopy also harbors the nocturnal northern flying squirrel and the golden mouse, which builds its nests up to thirty feet above the forest floor. Down there slither timber rattlers, copperheads, and a host of nonvenomous snakes.

Some of the many caves on the mountain are home to Virginia big-eared bats, whose ears are a quarter of the length of their four-inch-long bodies. They sleep suspended from the rock as many as 120 to the square foot.

The flora matches the diversity and spectacle of the fauna: Blue Ridge goldenrod, which blossoms in a spray of bright yellow flowers; bent avens—a species found on only three mountains—with furry buds that open into a white flower; and Heller's blazing star, a sixteen-inch-tall stalk crowned by a brilliant spike of lavender flowers half as long. The largest population of pink-shelled azalea in the world bursts into bloom each May, followed in June by the lavender-pink Catawba rhododendron. In the moss that grows on rocks at the foot of spruce trees, the spruce web moss spider, a minitarantula, weaves its funneled web—a reclusive arachnid fairly harmless to humans but deadly to trapped insects.[10]

Sapphire, emerald, ruby, garnet, tourmaline, amethyst, beryl, and fifty other gems have been mined in the vicinity, in addition to mica, zinc, kaolin, lead, feldspar, iron, copper, manganese, slate, greenstone, other building stone, and even gold.[11]

Grandfather Mountain is a wild paradise for trees, plants, and the creatures that abound there. But its commercially valuable natural resources were nearly its downfall.

Humans have coexisted with Grandfather Mountain for millennia. Nomadic Archaic peoples and Paleo-Indians moved through the mountain region for ten thousand years, percussion-flaking hard gneiss into projectile points, some of which were discovered at Attic Window Cave in 1882. Later the Cherokee and Siouan-speaking groups hunted the same territory.

The Scots-Irish came to the Appalachians in the 1700s, following the Great Wagon Road west from Philadelphia. Two of them, William Linville and his son, led a hunting party into country near what is now the Linville River, although exactly where they camped is lost to history. The *Pennsylvania Gazette* recorded their fate in an article published on October 9, 1766: "William Linvill, his son, and another young man, who had gone over the mountains at the head of the Yadkin river to hunt, were there surprised by some Indians. The father and son were both killed on the spot; the other young man got off, though much wounded, and arrived at his settlement, where he has since died." By 1778, the Linville name was attached to the river and its spectacular falls.[12]

Daniel Boone—who may have been among those who discovered the Linvilles' bodies—hunted the area and, even after moving across the Cumberland Gap, returned to a seasonal cabin on

Grandfather Mountain, where his nephew settled permanently. The naturalist William Bartram explored the country in 1776, followed a decade later by the botanist John Fraser, for whom the Fraser fir is named.[13]

An even more notable visitor, John Muir, founder of the Sierra Club, climbed Grandfather Mountain in September 1898, while he was recuperating from a severe bout of bronchitis that had racked him with fits of coughing and shortness of breath. Far from exhausting him, the climb exhilarated him. "The air has healed me," he wrote to his wife, Louisa. "I think I could walk ten miles and not be tired." He was so inspired by the panorama opening before him that a friend recounted him saying, "I couldn't hold in, and began to jump about and sing and glory in it all."[14]

A less well-known explorer was Worth Hamilton Weller, a seventeen-year-old high school student from Cincinnati. On a summer vacation trip to Grandfather Mountain in 1920, he encountered a clear-cut mountainside scarred by fire and washed out by torrential rain. Nonetheless, he climbed the ravaged slope and, turning over logs, discovered the gold-spotted salamander—a new species: *Plethodon welleri*. Weller graduated with honors and returned the following summer with a companion. In the midst of a collecting binge, he stumbled off an escarpment on the north slope and fell to his death.[15]

While the naturalists and botanists sought only discovery, more commercial-minded businessmen saw an opportunity for riches. In 1891, Samuel Kelsey, founder of Highlands, enlisted a partner, Donald MacRae of Wilmington, and formed the ironically named Linville Improvement Company (LIC). They built a tourist resort hotel at Linville at the northeast foot of Grandfather Mountain, then scraped out a serpentine toll road from Blowing Rock, the Yonahlossee Turnpike. The company bought sixteen thousand acres, including nearly all of Grandfather

Mountain, and proceeded to clear-cut the old-growth chestnut, locust, white pine, white and red oak, maple, cherry, and walnut. They logged so aggressively that soon the Linville area became known as Stumptown. By 1918, a narrow-gauge rail line, the Eastern and Western North Carolina Railroad, ran through Linville Gap for hauling out the timber.[16]

The company logged out the lower reaches first. By 1930, only the highest stands remained untouched. Harlan Kelsey, a botanist and environmental activist, had been for years working with the National Park Service (NPS) and the state to establish the Blue Ridge National Park on the site of Grandfather Mountain. He negotiated a price with the LIC, by then known as the Linville Company and controlled by Donald MacRae's

By the late 1950s, drivers could maneuver their cars to the summit of Linville Peak. Waiting at the top were the Mile-High Swinging Bridge and a visitors center called the Top Shop.

son, Hugh MacRae. The company insisted it be paid not just for the acreage but also for the remaining timber value of the land—making the asking price too exorbitant for the modest budget of the NPS. The deal fell through.

The company then hired a contractor, Will Smith, to clear-cut the higher trees—some of them two hundred feet tall and eight feet in diameter. Smith laid down eight miles of plank road, and the loggers went to work. When the rains came in August 1940, the bare mountain became a cataract, washing away the Grandfather community in a great landslide and flood.

By 1950, the NPS managed to buy 7,500 acres of Linville Gorge, in the vicinity of the clear-cut mountainside, for Pisgah National Forest.[17]

By the time Hugh MacRae's grandson, Hugh Morton, inherits Grandfather Mountain, he is keenly aware that it is a place for harvesting not timber but *wonder*. Nonetheless, the visitors will provide a steady income stream—and with the finished road to the top, in addition to the Mile-High Swinging Bridge and a stone visitors center called the Top Shop, Morton turns Grandfather Mountain into one of the most popular tourist destinations in the South.

In June 1953, he adds a new wrinkle: a sports car "Grandfather Mountain Hill Climb" up the steep hairpin curves, featuring Jaguars, Porsches, Renaults, and MGs, along with Fords, Chevys, and Buicks. And in MacRae Meadows, at the foot of the mountain, he carries on a tradition that dates to the 1920s: "Singing on the Mountain," an old-time gospel convention. His mother, Agnes MacRae Morton, and Donald MacDonald co-found the Highland Games and bring it to the mountain, where it becomes an annual three-day celebration of Gaelic culture with food, dancing, piping, fiddling, sheepdog trials, genealogy workshops, and competitions in traditional Scottish games

Against the backdrop of Grandfather, men tossed cabers at the inaugural Highland Games in 1956, and Governor Luther Hodges spoke at "Singing on the Mountain," now in its ninety-fifth year.

such as the hammer throw, tug-of-war, wrestling, and the caber toss—in which contestants hurl a nearly twenty-foot-long log into the air so that it spins and lands facing directly away from the tosser, as the old-time loggers were said to have thrown logs into streams.[18]

One last controversy boils up as the National Park Service plans to extend the "missing link" of the Blue Ridge Parkway over Grandfather Mountain by tunneling through the summit. Morton fights the plan for fifteen years, and at last a compromise route is reached: the S-shaped Linn Cove Viaduct, clinging to the side of the mountain without damaging it.

At the top of Grandfather Mountain, through the gorge between Linville and Second summits, the wind blows nearly constantly from the northwest, bending the limbs of the thickly forested spruce trees in a permanent "banner effect" pointing southeast. A hiker standing in the middle of the bridge can feel the wind pushing like an insistent hand and hear the cables hum as the wooden bridge deck rocks. Mornings in spring can bring both high winds and dense fog, so that, to a hiker peering into the encompassing clouds, the anchoring bridge towers on the cliffs are invisible and the sensation is that of sailing through the air, a kind of thrilling vertigo—an illusion, because it is the air, not the bridge, that is sweeping through the gorge but a powerful illusion, nevertheless, of flying headlong into timeless space.[19]

In 1950, children lined up for a kiddie matinee outside the new Carolina Theater in Lexington. After the original Carolina burned down in 1945, architect Erle Stillwell, who specialized in theaters and segregated spaces, designed a replacement that would accommodate white and Black patrons—separately.

CHAPTER

JUSTICE
IN
BLACK AND WHITE

As the spring semester opens at the Agricultural & Technical College of North Carolina in 1960, a group of Black freshmen holds regular meetings in their dormitory. It's a small campus, a place where everybody knows everybody else, and the meetings have a particular focus. Robert T. "Patt" Patterson, then a freshman majoring in engineering, remembers, "We talked about the things that as Black men we had to go through—going upstairs in movie houses, having to go to the back windows to purchase food. At any of these restaurants, they had a designated place for us. We started talking about it . . . and we decided that we were tired of doing that, and somebody was going to have to step forward."

Growing up in Laurinburg, a small town midway between Charlotte and Wilmington, Patterson would ask his father, "Why do we have to go upstairs?" The elder Patterson explained as best he could, mentioning a word that stuck in Patterson's mind: *segregation*. "And when I came to A&T and the subject came up, it really made me angry—although when we were demonstrating, we chose to do it in a nonviolent way. And so as a result of that, none of us got into any kind of altercation with any of the whites that we ran into."

On Monday, February 1, 1960, about a year after Dr. Martin Luther King delivers an inspiring speech in Greensboro, four of Patterson's classmates step forward: Ezell A. Blair Jr. (later Jibreel Khazan), Franklin E. McCain, Joseph A. McNeil, and David L. Richmond. They started downtown yesterday, but the seriousness of what they were about to do gave them pause, and at the last minute they called off their plan—a measure of how much moxie such an act of protest will require.[1]

This day, the four enter the downtown Woolworth, buy a few items—as local custom allows them to do—then sit on stools at the lunch counter, which local custom forbids. All are dressed professionally and behave courteously—in their discussions, they determined to emulate Gandhi and follow the path of nonviolence, figuring that will win them more allies. They already have made some allies in the white community, including Ralph Johns, a businessman who has contacted a news reporter to cover their protest.[2]

McCain, the tallest of the group, is wearing his Air Force ROTC uniform and dark-framed eyeglasses.[3] In truth, all four could have worn their uniforms—ROTC is required at A&T. If they are fit to defend their country, why can't they be served a sit-down meal? At first, as he takes his seat, McCain is filled with anxiety: what will happen when they try to order lunch at this whites-only counter? In an interview with National Public Radio, he recalls the moment that follows as one of almost sublime recognition: "Fifteen seconds after . . . I had the most wonderful feeling. I had a feeling of liberation, restored manhood. I had a natural high. And I truly felt almost invincible. Mind you, [I was] just sitting on a dumb stool and not having asked for service yet."

In that moment of quiet courage, he and his companions achieve a milestone—not just in their own lives but for a movement. "It's a feeling that I don't think that I'll ever be able to have again," he recalls. "It's the kind of thing that people pray for . . . and wish for all their lives and never experience it. And I felt as though I wouldn't have been cheated out of life had that been the end of my life at that second or that moment."

The manager, Clarence Harris, asks the young men to leave. When they do not, Harris directs the staff to ignore them. An older white woman is seated a few stools down from McCain, finishing a donut and cup of coffee, looking his way. He is sure she disapproves, wants him and the other Black students to get out. She stands up to leave, pauses behind McCain and McNeil, lays a hand on each of their shoulders, and says the last thing he expects to hear: "Boys, I am so proud of you, I only regret that you didn't do this ten years ago."[4]

The quiet protest of the four Black students is not just about equal service. It also calls attention to the wave of violence that has greeted Black soldiers home from the war, part of a long pattern of racial repression.

On Easter Sunday 1942, a Black soldier named Charles Banford walked into the Woolworth in downtown Wilson and ordered a hot dog at the lunch counter. When the manager saw him being served, he grabbed the hot dog away, shouting, "You know we don't sell to no n******!"[5]

The outcome could have been far worse for Banford. Between 1920 and 1943, thirty-seven Black citizens were lynched in North Carolina, and untold numbers of others suffered beatings and other acts of violence.

The struggle for racial equality became acute as Black soldiers returned from overseas military service after the war. They had become used to being respected and enjoying a greater measure of freedom than in their old hometowns. But returning home to the South, they encountered fierce and sometimes violent repression. In 1946, in Batesburg, South Carolina, Sergeant Isaac Woodward was manhandled off a bus by local police. The chief beat him so badly that Woodard suffered permanent blindness. That same year, two Black veterans and their wives—one of them pregnant—were pulled out of their cars near Monroe, Georgia, by a mob and shot multiple times with shotguns and pistols, their mutilated bodies left hanging from trees.[6]

President Harry S. Truman, who holds office from 1945 until 1953, has never been a proponent of racial equality. His slave-holding grandparents instilled the Confederate legacy deep in family lore. In 1911, courting his future wife, he wrote, "I think one man is just as good as another so long as he's honest and decent and not a n***** or a Chinaman." His foes accuse him of having paid the ten-dollar initiation fee to join the Ku Klux Klan early in his career, when it was a useful part of a political résumé in Missouri and other Midwestern states. But the list of new lynchings—especially those of veterans—appalls Truman, and he determines to do something dramatic. He issues an executive order, "Freedom From Fear," establishing the President's Committee on Civil Rights.

On June 29, 1947, Truman delivers an address to the NAACP—the first president to do so—from the steps of the Lincoln Memorial. "The only limit to an American's achievement should be his ability, his industry and his character," he declares. And lest anybody miss his point, he says bluntly: "When I say all Americans, I mean all Americans."[7]

Then on July 26, 1948—bucking lots of resistance inside his own Democratic Party—he signs the order officially desegregating the armed forces.

It is not just returning soldiers who encounter the harsh consequences of racial inequality. In October 1945, sixteen-year-old Marie Everett approached the concession stand at the Carolina Theater in Wilson—a city of some twenty thousand residents with the largest tobacco market in the world, served by the Atlantic Coast Line Railroad. Wilson still celebrated Confederate Memorial Day with a school holiday. Like most of the other theaters in town, the Carolina Theater admitted Black people but forced them to sit upstairs in a balcony known as the "crow's nest." As Everett stood next to her friend, who was buying popcorn, the white cashier shouted at her, demanding that she get in line.[8]

Everett replied that she was not in line, simply keeping her friend company and, as a parting shot, stuck out her tongue. According to Everett's friend, the cashier smacked Everett and grabbed her around the neck, as Everett tried to kick her way loose. Patrons called the police, while a Black soldier intervened, separating the two young women. The police arrested Everett for disorderly conduct, and a vindictive judge escalated that charge to simple assault. He sentenced her to be fined fifty dollars and serve three months in the county jail—three times the maximum allowable sentence.

Local NAACP officials hired a white lawyer to appeal. In court, one of two prosecutors reminded the jury that this trial was meant to show Black people "that the War is over"—that Black citizens, who by necessity may have enjoyed better employment and other advantages during the war years, had better remember their place. The all-white jury found her guilty, and this time the judge increased the sentence to six months of hard time—not in jail, but in the women's prison in Raleigh. It was patently illegal to send a minor there, so the prison officials returned her immediately to the county jail.

Eventually, Thurgood Marshall, counsel for the NAACP, took up her case. After he and his colleagues engineered the intervention of the State Commissioner of Paroles, Governor R. Gregg Cherry signed her parole. Everett was released in March 1946, having missed five months of high school.

Now other students find themselves on the front lines of the battle for civil rights. In 1896, the Supreme Court held in *Plessy v. Ferguson* that the doctrine of "separate but equal" was legal and adhered to the spirit of the Fourteenth Amendment of the Constitution: Thus segregation by race—including school segregation—was no longer just custom but the law of the land. That tenet is being challenged on multiple fronts.

Having been denied admission to the University of North Carolina's School of Law, Floyd McKissick joins a suit brought against the school in 1949—and, with Marshall's help, he wins. In 1951, McKissick, Harvey Beech, James Lassiter, and James Robert Walker become the first Black students at UNC.[9]

The next year, Marshall, acting with the NAACP Legal Defense Fund and Educational Fund, argues in *Brown v. Board of Education* (really the combination of five separate cases with the same legal principle at issue) that separate schools for Black students are inherently unequal.

In 1954, Chief Justice Earl Warren delivers the Supreme Court's unanimous—and momentous—decision: "We conclude that in the field of public education the doctrine of 'separate but equal' has no place. Separate educational facilities are inherently unequal."[10]

In 1951, Floyd McKissick became one of the first Black law students at UNC, paving the way for Dorothy Counts and Josephine Boyd, who, in 1957, desegregated Charlotte's Harding High and Greensboro Senior High (now Grimsley), respectively.

North Carolina governor William Umstead announces he is "terribly disappointed" with the ruling. H. C. West, a statistician with the State Board of Education, laments the timing, declaring that the state was "within approximately $36,591,171 of establishing parity between white and Negro public schools. Sanford Martin, formerly the editor of the *Winston-Salem Journal* and the *Twin City Sentinel* and member of the State Board of Education, writes, "If the Negroes are wise, I think they will help solve our school problem by voluntary segregation."[11]

A majority of the state's congressional delegation signs the so-called "Southern Manifesto," authored by North Carolina senator Sam Ervin Jr., which declares that Southern states will resist forced integration by any lawful means.[12]

The North Carolina legislature reacts with a retrograde action to delay desegregation for as long as possible. Speaker of the House Thomas J. Pearsall of Rocky Mount chairs a Special Advisory Committee on Education and asserts, "We are of the unanimous opinion that the people of North Carolina will not support mixed schools. . . . We think it is also true that children do best when in school with children of their own race."[13]

Pearsall's committee crafts legislation that comes to be known as the Pearsall Plan. Among other provisions, it specifies the following: Local districts will control the assignment of students to schools; students assigned to an integrated school against their wishes are excused from attending; and if such students wish to attend a private school, the state will pay their tuition. The plan also includes an explicit "resolution of condemnation and protest" against the *Brown* decision. In a statewide referendum in 1956, more than 80 percent of voters approve the Pearsall Plan. White public schools in Charlotte, Greensboro, and Winston-Salem enroll some Black students; students in other districts sue for inclusion. Ten years after the *Brown* decision, just one out of a hundred Black students attends a desegregated school.[14]

On June 23, 1957, The Reverend Douglas Moore leads a group of African Americans in staging a sit-in at the Royal Ice Cream Company in Durham. The protesters are arrested. For legal counsel, Moore turns to a young lawyer who is by now well versed in the fight for desegregation, Floyd McKissick.

The tide is turning, ever so slowly, toward equality, and it engulfs the lunch counter crowd of the Greensboro Woolworth in 1960.

On the second day of the Greensboro sit-in, (left to right) Joseph A. McNeil and Franklin E. McCain were joined by more A&T students, including William Smith and Clarence Henderson, at Woolworth's whites-only lunch counter.

The first sit-in at Woolworth lasts until closing. The four young men leave still hungry. The next day, more students join them—including Patterson, the engineering major. He is considering changing his major to economics, but his involvement in the civil rights protests eventually causes the chair of that department to become concerned for his academic progress. "She called me in," Patterson recounts. "She said, 'I admire what you're doing, but you're going to open up doors you're not going to be able to walk in yourself . . . you need to get your degree—if you're going to take advantage of any of these things that are going to come out of this.'"

His father agrees, but he also commends his son's passion for justice. He tells him, "I'm not going to even try to tell you that what you're doing is wrong. . . . If my generation had had any guts, you all wouldn't have had to do it." Patterson earns his economics degree a year behind schedule.

Meanwhile, the protest gathers strength. Patterson remembers, "The A&T football team had won the conference championship that year, and all of the guys on the football team put on their CIAA championship jackets and they were kind of the people that were protecting us the first week or so."

The protest—now a movement—spreads to other lunch counters, and crowds of angry white men show up to harass and threaten the protesters. By Thursday, the A&T protesters are joined by students from Bennett, a nearby college for Black women. Newspaper reporters and a television news crew cover the event. In the following days, students from Dudley High School, Guilford College, and the Women's College of the University of North Carolina (now UNC-Greensboro) also show up. By Saturday, as many as a thousand people are protesting the whites-only policy—and sit-ins have spread to Woolworth stores in Durham, Winston-Salem, and Charlotte.

The choice of Woolworth—followed by Kress and K&W Cafeterias—is intentional, according to Patterson: "We deliberately picked the national firms because they had integrated facilities elsewhere . . . we figured it would spread faster that way."

Before long, Captain William Jackson of the Greensboro Police visits campus and asks the young men to notify his department whenever a protest is planned. Thereafter, the police escort the protesters to and from downtown, thus forestalling confrontations with white counterprotesters—and any violent pushback from the Ku Klux Klan, which, fortunately, remains absent from the scene.

Not until July 25, 1960, does the Greensboro Woolworth at last concede. The same manager who has stubbornly refused to serve African Americans for more than six months invites four Black employees to sit at the counter. They trade their uniforms for street clothes and enjoy the first meals served to Black patrons. The segregation that has ruled North Carolina's eating establishments has been broken—soon many lunch counters serve Black and white diners equally, although some shut down to avoid the choice.

The nonviolent sit-in becomes one of the most successful tactics of the entire Civil Rights movement, spreading across the South to Nashville, Atlanta, and Richmond.[15]

For North Carolina, the Woolworth sit-in signals the beginning, not the end, of the newly energized struggle for civil rights. Patterson never thought about making history. The names of many of those like him who stepped forward are never celebrated, but their goal was never notoriety. "I wasn't out there for that reason," he says. "My reason totally was to do what I could to make things better for black folks."

The A&T students and their supporters open a door and walk through it to a new era.

As commercial aviation captures the public's imagination, conditions are just right for a North Carolina airline—born and bred in Winston-Salem—to take off.

CHAPTER

PIEDMONT AIRLINES SETS THE PACE

Two boys, two airplanes, four miles and seven years apart. Separated by time and a little distance, the boys stare up at the empty skies above Winston-Salem. Then the planes come into sight: circling, dipping low—then swooping into a glide path, bumping down on the ground, rolling to a stop. For each boy, it is a life-changing event that will one day connect them in a daring enterprise.

The first boy is thirteen-year-old Richard J. "Dick" Reynolds Jr., son of the recently deceased tobacco magnate R. J. Reynolds, watching along with his little brother, Smith, his sisters, and his mother. The Avro 504K two-seater biplane touches down on the front lawn of the great estate his father built just before his death two years before, called Reynolda.

Out of the open cockpit climb Harry J. Runser and Roscoe Turner, barnstorming pilots outfitted in the rakish uniform of the Army Air Corps, complete with Sam Browne belts and high boots. Turner is the taller—handsome, with a flashing smile and waxed moustache. The year is 1920.

Dick is entranced by the airplane, and the moment ignites a lifelong passion for flying.[1]

The second boy is Tom Davis, nine years old, part of a crowd of twenty-five thousand who have come out to Miller Field to see the famous Lone Eagle, Charles Lindbergh. The date is October 14, 1927—just months after Lindbergh became the first solo aviator to fly nonstop across the Atlantic Ocean. Davis never forgets that day: "I think Lindbergh was largely responsible for my interest in flying," he recalls many years later.[2]

He's come to the airport with his father, Egbert L. Davis, who managed the Chicago sales force for R. J. Reynolds Tobacco that made Camel cigarettes a household brand—and reaped a fortune for the company. Lindbergh is an apostle for aviation. Planes have been used to make war and to entertain, and now he exhorts the admiring crowd to recognize the possibilities of commercial aviation—"conducting a progressive air program for your city in order to keep your city in the foreground of American aeronautics."

Dick Reynolds takes up flying as a young man, as does his younger brother Smith. He founds Reynolds Aviation at Miller Field—a "fixed base" operation that repairs and sells planes and conducts flying lessons. Then he buys Curtiss Field on Long Island, New York, where Lindbergh hangered his plane for his historic flight. He hires Lewin S. "Mac" McGinnis, Lindbergh's sometime mechanic and a flying instructor, and launches a passenger carrier, Reynolds Airways, in 1927. Its first scheduled flight takes off from Curtiss Field in a driving rainstorm—and crashes in a New Jersey orchard. Five passengers, the pilot, and the mechanic are killed, and Reynolds moves his operation back to Winston-Salem, renaming it Reynolds Aviation and, later, Camel City Flying Service.[3]

Smith Reynolds racks up aviation records of his own. At sixteen, he earns his transport pilot's license—and in 1930 he sets an unofficial speed record between New York and Los Angles, then covers a six-thousand-mile route across Europe and Asia in 1931. But in 1932, recently married, having just purchased a new airplane, he returns to Reynolda. After a raucous, late-night party, the watchman discovers him unconscious on the sleeping porch, a bullet wound to the right temple. His wife Libby—several years older than he—is indicted for murder, along with a friend, Albert Walker, but the case never comes to trial and is dismissed by many as a suicide.[4]

Shaken by his brother's death, Dick Reynolds loses his passion for flying.

Meanwhile, Tom Davis grows up playing with a balsa wood model of *Spirit of St. Louis* propelled by a rubber band, gets his first ride in an airplane at age eleven. He saves his allowance to take flying lessons from McGinnis—now based in Winston-Salem—and solos at age sixteen in a canvas-covered two-seater Taylor Cub with a thirty-seven-horsepower engine. To alleviate his chronic asthma, he goes out West, enrolling at the University of Arizona—where he soon loses interest in his premed studies and spends his time flying above the desert and giving flying lessons for a dollar an hour.

He returns home determined to make his mark in aviation, starting as an aircraft salesman with Camel City. With his father's support, he buys a significant share of Camel City from Dick Reynolds. He gradually increases his stake until he is majority owner and, in 1940, changes the name to Piedmont Aviation. During the war, the company enjoys a lucrative government contract for training pilots, but at war's end, he decides on a bold move: he will create his own airline.

By now Piedmont has more than fifty employees counting on him. Davis is not striking in appearance—he is lean, with an angular face, long nose, high forehead, and receding hairline. He is friendly and approachable rather than imperious and would rather hang out with the mechanics in the hangar than in the boardroom. He earns his employees' confidence for his calm demeanor in a crisis, his wide and deep knowledge of every aspect of aviation, his hands-on approach to business, and his personal integrity.

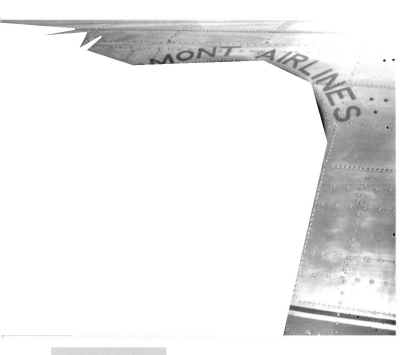

By 1954, Winston-Salem's Smith Reynolds Airport had evolved since its early days as Miller Field. It served as Piedmont's headquarters, and founder Tom Davis kept an office there even after USAir bought the airline in 1989.

He names the new venture Piedmont Airlines, an echo of the nineteenth-century railroad called the Piedmont Air Line, which ran between Richmond and Atlanta and advertised a ride as smooth as air. Davis's "coaches" will ride on *real* air. To keep costs down—always a concern—he leases and buys wartime-surplus DC-3s, proven workhorses that are easily converted to passenger planes, though they are unpressurized and hard to keep heated in flight. But as Harold Dobbins, who will copilot the first commercial flight, makes clear, Davis values safety above all else: "Being a pilot, he was very much interested in safety. He would spend money in the cockpit and leave passengers in a hard seat."[5]

So Piedmont mechanics rebuild each plane to their exacting standards, standardizing cockpit instruments, stripping each fuselage down to bare metal and repainting it red, white, and blue.

For Piedmont's tailfin logo, Davis chooses the distinctive "Speedbird" with three upright red tail feathers. He calls his aircraft "Pacemakers": "From the very beginning," he writes, "our motto has been 'Piedmont Sets the Pace.' That's what we call our airplanes, Pacemakers." Each plane's name is painted on the captain's side of the nose: *Buckeye Pacemaker, Tidewater Pacemaker, Appalachian Pacemaker.*[6]

Davis selects his flight crews from the abundance of military veteran pilots—not the daredevils, but the steady men who can handle the routine of fixed schedules and present the company in its best light.

From the start, he determines that Piedmont will hire North Carolinians whenever possible—as pilots, mechanics, stewardesses, pursers, station agents—and buy equipment and materials from in-state companies. But in this age of segregation, he hires only white people to work in the cabin or man the cockpit. Across the South, airports remain segregated, but the cabins of airliners are not—there is no practical way to do it and satisfy safety regulations.[7]

Davis markets 675,000 shares of stock to North Carolinians, with the warning that the venture is risky. By his retirement, each $1 share will pay back $60.

The result is a legacy of extraordinary esprit de corps and mutual loyalty between Davis and his employees that will last as long as the airline. Piedmont is awarded Route 87, which originates in Wilmington, continues through stations across North Carolina, and reaches to Virginia, West Virginia, Kentucky, Tennessee, and Ohio. With it comes a contract to carry the U.S. Mail—crucial to the airline's financial stability.

Two major carriers—Delta and Eastern—and one Charlotte-based carrier, State Airlines, challenge Piedmont's award, and litigation nearly sinks Piedmont before it can start flying, reaching as far as the United States Supreme Court. At last, on February 20, 1948, after weather delays have postponed the original Valentine's Day inaugural, Tom Davis personally flies the *Kanawha River Pacemaker* to Wilmington to start the official first flight—a bellwether success.

As Pacemakers deliver their passengers on time and with signature courtesy, these passengers become nearly as effusive in their loyalty to Piedmont as are crew and ground employees. The Piedmont Airlines newsletter for August 21, 1948, includes a letter from Margaret B. Colvert, who flew to Johnson City, Tennessee, because of the death of her brother: "It was my first trip by air, and even though my mission was a sad one to me, personally, I wanted to tell you that the trip was the most pleasant and easiest one I have ever made."[8]

Davis personally oversees all the myriad details of the airline, coaxing his employees to excellence through his personal charm and conversational reports. The December 22, 1948, newsletter contains the "November Delay Report": "You fellows take a look at the delay report sent to all stations recently by Mr. Turbiville and I am sure that you will join me in congratulating GSB

[Greensboro]. No delays at that station for the month. DAN [Danville] is also to be congratulated as they only had a total of 3 minutes of time on the ground, and I am sure that those 3 minutes were used to the fullest advantage. Yes sir, those are two mighty good records. Who else can do as well?"[9]

Despite the hospitality service in the cabin, the addition of in-flight lounges, and the trappings of living-room comfort, passenger aviation is just finding its stride, and flying can still be dangerous. In December 1948, Captain H. H. Hutchison has just taken off from the Tri-City (Bristol–Kingsport–Johnson City) airport in Tennessee enroute to Cincinnati when first one engine and then the second sputters out. He is forced to make an emergency landing in a nearby field. The hard landing "shook loose" his landing gear. As darkness comes on, crewmen build a fire to warm passengers as they await transport back to the airport.[10]

In a bizarre incident on June 10, 1956, a graveyard worker at Zion Baptist Church in Shelby named Luther Haynes reports, "I heard a loud swoosh. Then it sounded like an explosion." What he heard was a passenger falling 6,500 feet from the Charlotte-to-Ashville *Tidewater Pacemaker* and hitting the ground, killed on impact with the graveyard. His name is Oren Ase Pruitt, a chef traveling with his new bride. Apparently, while trying to find the restroom, he opened instead the rear door of the aircraft and was sucked out into the slipstream. Pruitt is Piedmont's first fatality.[11]

The Associated Press reports, "The Pruitts, married Tuesday in York, S.C., were on their honeymoon to Asheville to meet Mrs. Pruitt's parents.

"Mrs. Pruitt, under a doctor's care at her parents' home, said her husband got up to go to the men's room. She added: 'I heard—it was a little while after that—a big whoosh. The wind was screaming in. Somebody said the door had blown off.

"'I thought Oren was still in the men's room. Nobody got up. I was afraid to look back there. And then a stewardess came to my seat and sat down beside me. I knew then. Nobody ever told me anything. I don't know what happened. I just know he was gone.'"[12]

Still, Piedmont maintains a remarkable safety record, given that its Pacemakers fly over rugged Appalachian terrain along routes buffeted by towering summer thunderstorms and ambushed by winter snowstorms, into airports tucked between ridges in bowls that often fill with soupy fog. Time and again, Piedmont's well-trained pilots—many with a history of combat flying experience—manage safe landings despite ominous weather, slick runways, faulty landing gear, or failed engines.

But Piedmont's decade-long run of good fortune ends on the night before Halloween, 1959. Piedmont Flight 349, the *Buckeye Pacemaker* from Washington, D.C., carrying twenty-four passengers and three crew members, is on final instrument approach to Charlottesville in a foggy drizzle but, unaccountably and unbeknownst to the flight crew, is almost eight miles off course. It slams into Buck's Elbow Mountain, just west of Charlottesville in Crozet. Sudden impact at a speed of more than 160 miles per hour tears the plane apart, killing everybody aboard—except one man. Phil Bradley missed an earlier flight and took the last open seat on this one—the right rear seat. Bradley, a decorated D-Day veteran, hears "a tremendous crunching of metal, then everything went black"—as the wings shear off trees and he instinctively ducks. Then he is catapulted through a hole in the fuselage some sixty-five feet, still strapped into his seat. "The next thing I knew I was trying to get dirt and leaves out of my mouth."

In the midst of the catastrophe, he sees a vision of Jesus Christ. "He looked at me and said, 'Be concerned not, I will be with you always,'" he later tells an interviewer. Bodies are scattered across the mountainside—along with at least one crew member and several passengers who likely survived impact but now succumb to their injuries. Bradley spends Halloween lying in the drizzly cold, watching as a bear and her cub wander past. The pain from his dislocated hip and injured feet keep him awake. He shouts himself hoarse, then prays. Sunday dawn illuminates a wake of turkey vultures gathering in the trees around him. Later that day, thirty-five hours after the crash, rescuers—including Zeke Saunders, vice president of Piedmont—find him. They sedate him and carry him to the summit, from where he can be safely airlifted to a hospital.

Piedmont was legendary for its punctuality and friendly service. Once aboard, pursers passed out magazines—and, if passengers were lucky, Krispy Kreme doughnuts.

Piedmont concludes that an unauthorized homing beacon in Pennsylvania interfered with the navigation of Flight 349, pulling it off course. The Civil Aeronautics Board (CAB) disagrees, blaming thirty-two-year-old Captain George Lavrinc based on the fact that he had received psychotherapy and taken psychotropic medications: "The consensus is that Captain Levrinc was so heavily burdened with mental and emotional problems that he should have been relieved of the strain of flight duty while undergoing treatment for his condition. The condition was such that preoccupation with his problems could well have lowered his standard of performance during instrument flight."[13]

Piedmont recovers, earning an admirable safety record in the years to come. From 1948 until 1989, when it is acquired by USAir and launches its last flight as Piedmont, it suffers just four major crashes. To the finish, the airline started by Tom Davis retains the stubborn loyalty of its employees and passengers.

The day of Piedmont Airlines' first flight from Wilmington signals the end of one era and the beginning of another: Earlier in February 1948, Orville Wright died, as did Captain John T. Daniels, the last surviving member of the lifeboat crew that helped the Wrights launch their first *Flyer* on the sands of Kill Devil Hills at Kitty Hawk.

The day of the inaugural Piedmont flight dawns clear and cold. All except one passenger are nonpaying VIPs. True to form, Davis lets the single paying passenger board first. He pays $34.50 for the round-trip fare from Wilmington to Cincinnati. The passenger is Bill Turner—brother to Roscoe Turner, the dashing barnstormer who landed his biplane on the lawn at Reynolda in 1920, inspiring Dick Reynolds to take to the air.

Lumbee handcrafts often feature the "Pine Cone Patchwork" design, created in the late 1800s to resemble the bottom of a longleaf pine cone. The insignia is a common sight at the annual Lumbee Homecoming and Powwow, including on the traditional regalia worn by Madison Locklear during the intertribal dance.

CHAPTER

THE
LUMBEE FIND
RECOGNITION

Through the early decades of the twentieth century, the Lumbee Indians are not much known outside of Robeson County in the southeastern part of the state—though their forebears settled there by at least 1754, when an agent for colonial governor Arthur Dobbs discovered some fifty families living at the headwaters of the Little Pee Dee. His description was less than flattering: "a lawless people, [who] possess the Lands without patent or paying any quit rents." Thus began a long history with white settlers during which the Lumbee struggled to gain respect.[1]

Their lineage is a matter of contention, including perhaps the gray-eyed Hatteras—or Hattorask—Indians, the Tuscarora, the Saponi, the Cheraws, the Cape Fear Indians. White people, so-called free persons of color, and escaped formerly enslaved Black people intermarried with them. Some believe they are descended from the settlers of Sir Walter Raleigh's Lost Colony of Roanoke Island—a much-contested addition to the myth of the disappeared colonists. In many ways, the Lumbee are unlike most other American Indian tribes. They are one of the few tribes never to have been confined to a reservation. Their native language—Algonkian, Siouan, or Iroquoian—has long since disappeared from living memory. And their appearance—skin tone and hair color—varies across a wide range, including many fair-haired, pale-skinned Lumbee. They mainly adhere to the Southern Baptist or Methodist faith.[2]

Even their name is hard to fix. In 1885, the North Carolina Legislature recognized the tribe and named them Croatan Indians. In 1910 the U.S. House of Representatives tried—unsuccessfully—to rename them the Cherokee. The following year, the state legislature designated them Indians of Robeson County. In 1913, the state legislature changed their name yet again to the Cherokee Indians of Robeson County, but the U.S. Senate failed to pass a bill recognizing the name. The U.S. House tried again, without success, to enroll them as Cheraw or Cherokee. The U.S. Senate pursued the idea of renaming them Siouan Indians—again, to no avail. At last, in 1953, the North Carolina Legislature officially grants them the name chosen by tribal ballot: the Lumbee Indians of North Carolina, after the Lumber River, which runs through their home county. Three years later, the federal Lumbee Act codifies the name, but denies government benefits to the tribe.[3]

The Lumbee have long been treated as second-class citizens—and have fought for their rights just as long. In 1835, the state constitution took away their right to vote or own firearms. During the Civil War, Lumbees were conscripted into hard labor to build Confederate works along the Cape Fear River, including massive Fort Fisher. A Lumbee farmer named Allen Lowry and his family were accused of leading a resistance movement, stealing guns, aiding escaped U.S. Army prisoners and Confederate deserters, and hiding in swamps to avoid conscription. When the Home Guard executed Lowry and his eldest son, William, in 1865, a younger son, Henry Berry Lowry, continued the fight, still an outlaw long after war's end. The Lowry band successfully eluded an armed force sent to capture them in 1870. When the N.C. legislature offered a bounty on Henry Berry Lowry's head, another militia force tracked the band and captured several members, but Henry Berry again proved impossible to catch. He led a final raid on Lumberton in 1872, then disappeared into legend.[4]

As late as the 1950s, the thirty thousand Lumbee in Robeson County endure three-way segregation and bigotry. The movie house in Lumberton seats white patrons downstairs. Upstairs, Black and Lumbee patrons are required to sit in separate sections, fenced off by a barrier of chicken wire. Their children attend separate schools. Verdia Locklear later recalls those days for an interviewer: "You don't know what it's like for you to go into a drug store—now, I'm telling you my experience—go into the drug store, you're sick, and you ask for a fountain Coke . . . And I got the fountain Coke and I couldn't . . . they wouldn't let me sit down. And I passed out."[5]

In 1958, the Lumbee are about to become nationally famous—not for their culture or heritage or battle for tribal recognition—but for another kind of battle altogether, a principled fight against a familiar foe: the Ku Klux Klan. Verdia Locklear is twenty-four years old, a wife and expectant mother, when she reads in the *Robesonian* that the Klan intends to stage a rally in Maxton on January 18.

The organizer is the Grand Wizard of the KKK from Marion, South Carolina, James W. "Catfish" Cole—a heavy-browed man with a thin face, receding dark hair, and a scraggly goatee. His stated purpose is to "put the Indians in their place and to end race-mixing." His followers have burned crosses in the yards of a Lumbee family that moved into a white neighborhood and a Native American woman said to be dating a white man.[6]

But Cole and his fellow Klansmen haven't reckoned on the determination of the Lumbee, who organize immediately to disrupt the rally. "The first thing they'd say, be sure you got your pistol, and if you don't have a pistol, carry your rifle," Locklear says. Accompanied by her husband, Wiley, she carries her pistol to the field near Hayes Pond, where a stage has been erected, lit by a single generator-powered bulb. In the darkness fronting the stage and in the perimeter surrounding it, some 350 armed members of the Lumbee Tribe hunker down, awaiting their cue.

Catfish Cole takes the stage. "When he started talking on the microphone, they started shooting then," Locklear recounts. One of the first shots smashes the light bulb. "It was dark. It was *dark*," she says. "Wiley didn't get—my husband—he didn't get too far from me, 'cause all of us was shooting. They didn't let him [Cole] talk, period. He got gone."

The Lumbees rush the stage and swarm over the Klansmen, two of whom are wounded by buckshot. Taken by surprise, the Klansmen are routed. Locklear continues, "They were shocked, 'cause they had no dreams that we would be there like we were." The Lumbees take the crosses the Klansmen were intending to burn and make a bonfire of their own near the railroad. The Lumbees' stand turns into a jubilant celebration that goes on until four o'clock in the morning.

The Lumbee contingent includes Charlie Warriax and Simeon Oxendine—a veteran who flew twenty-four bombing missions over Germany as a waist gunner in a B-17, known as a man who is fearless. He and Warriax seize the Klan's white banner—emblazoned with KKK—and clown around for a photographer, wrapping themselves in it, grinning and winking for the camera.

The picture is featured in *Life* magazine, along with a story about what is already being called the Battle of Hayes Pond—"Bad Medicine for The Klan—North Carolina Indians break up Ku Kluxers' anti-Indian meeting."[7]

Cole and his Klan associate, James Martin, are arrested for inciting a riot. Martin is tried in the Maxton Recorders' Court, where the presiding judge is Lacy Maynor, a Lumbee. He scolds Martin before passing sentence: "You came into a community with guns, where there was a very happy and contented group of people. We don't go along with violence. . . . We can't understand why you want to come here and bring discord." Martin gets six months to a year in prison. Once Cole is extradited from South Carolina, he faces trial in Robeson County Superior Court. He earns a sentence of eighteen months to two years.[8]

After the Battle of Hayes Pond (above), Judge Lacy Maynor, a Lumbee, presided over the trial of Klansman James Martin.

Malvina Reynolds, the daughter of Jewish Hungarian immigrants who became a folk singer and labor activist—and who herself has been harassed by the Klan—memorializes the event in a satirical ballad, "The Battle of Maxton Field." In one of the nine verses, she sings:

> *Our histories will long record*
> *That perilous advance,*
> *When many a Klansman left the field*
> *With buckshot in his pants.*[9]

From 1939 to 1953, Pembroke State College—now UNC Pembroke—was the country's only four-year state college for Native Americans. By the '50s, school spirit was strong, including new traditions like a field day for Robeson County schools and familiar landmarks like the "Old Main" building and a stone arrowhead marker.

Not only have the Lumbee routed the Klan—they have turned it into an object of ridicule. But the true measure of Lumbee progress is the tribe's increasing political power. Some four months after the Klan is sent packing, Tracy Sampson is elected as Robeson County's first Lumbee Indian commissioner. Soon other Lumbees assume important leadership roles beyond the tribe, on the board of education and as president of Pembroke State College.

In 1962, a delegation of thirty-two Native Americans presents to President John F. Kennedy the *Declaration of Indian Purpose*. One of those standing with the president at the White House is a young staff member for the U.S. Senate Subcommittee on Constitutional Rights under Senator Sam Ervin: Dr. Helen Maynor Scheirbeck of Lumberton—daughter of Judge Lacy Maynor.[10]

Inspired by her father's example of activism in pursuit of justice, Sheirbeck goes on to become perhaps the best-known advocate in the nation for the rights of Native Americans to control their own communities, working on reservations around the country and later as the director of the Office of Indian Education of the U.S. Department of Health, Education, and Welfare in Washington, D.C. She becomes a tireless advocate for education as a way of improving the lives of Native peoples. She helps draft the Indian Education Act of 1975 and champions the Tribally Controlled Community College Assistance Act of 1978. She carries the fight for the rights of the Lumbee—and all other Native tribes—far beyond Robeson County and into the halls of Congress.

An early planning
meeting for the
Research Triangle Park.

CHAPTER

THE **SHAPE** OF **THINGS** TO **COME**

I t is the gift of some remarkable people to be able to see a thing entire where nothing yet exists. And sometimes a great enterprise comes together when several such people hold competing visions but manage to reconcile them into a single viable reality.

Such enterprises may not be as glamorous or exciting as rescuing a priceless mountain from developers or launching a pioneering airline. They require many hours of committee meetings, patient research, reasoned arguments, and persuasion—bringing together people with allied interests, changing the minds of naysayers, working quietly for years without fanfare to accomplish something extraordinary that following generations will take for granted. Such is the origin of Research Triangle Park.

Dr. Howard Washington Odum, a renowned sociologist and founder of the University of North Carolina Institute for Research in Social Science with nearly three decades of faculty service, initially proposes founding a research institute in the Piedmont, a nexus of cooperation between the three universities—North Carolina State, Duke, and UNC Chapel Hill—to explore issues related to the American South. His idea languishes in the conservative hierarchy of the universities, what UNC System president Gordon Gray confides with some frustration to his assistant, William Friday, is "administrative chaos." Gray attempts to reform the governance of the consolidated university with the help of consultants hired partly through a Ford Foundation grant. Professor Odum takes a leading role, convening a series of All-University Conferences to find areas of cooperation—but he dies in 1954 with his vision for a research institute unfulfilled.[1]

The problem is bigger than just getting the universities to cooperate. Somehow an essential link is missing between higher education and the real-world prospects for graduates in the state's languishing economy. Too many of North Carolina's best-educated citizens have been leaving for better opportunities in more progressive places. The state's Department of Commerce dramatizes this plight in a 1954 film depicting resigned parents sending their grown child off on a train. The voiceover intones, "Every year, many of our best educated young people leave to find a living elsewhere. Of all our state's resources these young people are the most valuable, and we're still losing them by the thousands."[2]

At the same time, industrial production after the war is slacking off—and the state heads into recession in 1957.

In the early 1950s, Romeo Guest relocates his industrial contracting firm to Greensboro. He begins energetic efforts to lure companies from other states to North Carolina and the Southeast, where he hopes to build their factories. He is not very successful but conceives a new angle, capitalizing on the presence of the three world-class universities, to create what he calls "a golden triangle of research." Unlike Odum, he does not envision an institute of pure research but rather a pragmatic engine for promoting business and economic growth—a cluster of enterprises, loosely aligned, taking full advantage of the wide and deep expertise concentrated in the three universities to conduct targeted research to develop new technologies. As a student at the Massachusetts Institute of Technology, he saw how university collaboration with business produced the futuristic tech development corridor along Route 128 in Massachusetts.[3]

Research Triangle Park's earliest visionaries had different objectives—UNC professor Howard Odum dreamed of an institute of pure research, while contractor Romeo Guest saw a business opportunity. But their shared goal turned out to be a boon for the whole state.

He writes, "We had three major universities all giving doctor-ate degrees, all doing research, all well financed, and all within a very short distance of each other. In fact, they appeared to me to sort of run together and be one [great] intellectual complex where research could be carried on with the brains already there. In other words, we had the brains—all we needed was the money and a spark to set us off."[4]

He coins the magic words: *Research Triangle*. The concept now comes alive in the imaginations of the leaders who can make it happen. And with the nation deep in the Cold War with the Soviet Union, Guest understands that some of that neces-sary capital can be gotten directly from the U.S. government, which is heavily funding scientific research. He writes to his assistant, Phyllis Branch, "I have heard that MIT has research grants from the government through industry amounting to approximately $5 million per year and that California institu-tions are similarly loaded."[5]

Research Triangle Park's special draw is embedded in its very name—the geographic triangle of open land formed by the three robust research universities, each located in a metropolitan area. The word *triangle* also signifies that three important entities need to work together to make it a reality: business, the uni-versities, and the state.[6]

In 1951, Guest floats the idea of a Research Triangle Park (RTP) to Brandon Hodges, the state treasurer, and Walter Harp-er, a member of the state board of conservation and develop-ment. Both are receptive. But though the term has a nice ring to it, no one can quite figure out how to connect the universities and private enterprise. Their structures, goals, and cultures are vastly different—even contradictory.

The many moving parts confound the for-profit venture: Universities shy about partnering with private enterprise. Law-makers wary of favoring certain companies over others. Even the reluctance of some of those private companies to relocate their operations in an untried arrangement lacking roads and other essential infrastructure in a state whose primary and secondary education systems are the mirror opposites of its universities: poor rather than excellent—not a draw for educated workers with families.

All three universities' leaders share the same misgiving: They do not want to compromise their teaching mission. Guest, who has solicited support from business and political leaders, has not yet won the favor of the very universities featured in his own brochure, titled "Conditioned for Research," which offers the services of university researchers outright to companies who would relocate to the state.

The brochure's promise elicits a backlash from some of the most important leaders on campus—the very people whose co-operation he will need. William D. "Billy" Carmichael, controller of the Consolidated UNC System and a man known for his wit, tells him, "Let me see, Romeo, if I really understand what we're talking about here—you want the professors here and all of us to be the prostitutes and you're going to be the pimp."[7]

But Guest keeps on meeting with those in a position to make the venture possible: Robert M. Hanes, president of Wachovia bank; Hanes's successor, Chairman Archie K. Davis; and Governor Luther Hodges, the son of a mill worker in Spray (now Eden), who himself worked for a textile mill as a boy. Hodges is energetically probusiness.[8]

The recession of 1957–58 has hit hard, and Governor Hodges is determined to attract new businesses to the state—and succeeds: each of the last three years of the decade exceeds its predecessor in new investment, with more than a quarter billion dollars pumped into the state's economy in 1959–60.[9]

Hodges becomes the critical supporter, for commitment from the state will reassure chary investors that RTP is a long-term enterprise. Hodges invites delegations from all three universities to a luncheon at the governor's mansion in February 1955, signaling his intention to make the realization of RTP one of the top goals of his administration. In a speech announcing that commitment, he explains that "two thirds of these young people trained in sciences at these three institutions are forced to leave North Carolina, and indeed the entire South, to find suitable employment."[10]

North Carolina is an unlikely place to attract educated professionals and their families. The state has generally been hostile to unions, and low-wage industrial jobs and labor-intensive farming have long driven its economy. In 1953, its annual per capita wage is just two-thirds the national average—and forty-seventh among the contiguous states.[11]

The state has actively resisted integration of both public schools and public universities. It is not a center of innovation.

From the start, Davis, the new head of Wachovia, doesn't think the for-profit enterprise makes sense, and he tells Governor Hodges so: "If this indeed was designed for public service, then it would be much easier to raise money from corporations and institutions and the like, who were interested in serving the state of North Carolina, by making a contribution."[12]

As early as July 1955, Professor Paul Gross, vice president of education at Duke, proposes the idea for an institute that bridges the gap between basic university research and industrial research. When William Friday succeeds Gray as president of UNC, he is firmly committed to the notion of such a research institute—but only if it conforms to his vision of serving the public good. There is a vigorous debate about just what its mission should be: Governor Hodges wants an economic engine; Romeo Guest and other businessmen want primarily a land-development enterprise. Friday insists that any research institute must be controlled by the universities, separate from the business-oriented Research Triangle Park Foundation.

Ultimately Friday's plan is accepted—RTP will be a hybrid of private enterprise and public interest, with an independent research institute allied with all three universities and a business park controlled by the foundation. Everyone agrees on one thing: whatever RTP is at its inception, it must grow and become both larger and more significant over time. It is a bet on the future.[13]

In 1956, the Research Triangle Committee is formed, incorporated as a nonprofit and headed by Odum's protégé, Professor George Simpson. Thus begins the turn from a for-profit venture into a nonprofit collaboration.[1]

Now that he can solicit donations toward the greater public good, rather than risky investment, Davis displays a genius for fundraising, coming up with $1.5 million to get the project started.[1]

Simpson articulates their mission: "The Research Triangle Committee, while it is a private nonprofit corporation, is essentially a public agency. This is true for several reasons. First, its essential control must invariably be located in the desires and feelings of the institutions. Second, its operations are supported by contributions from the public at large, notably people from Chapel Hill, Durham, and Raleigh. Third, our objective is the service of all the state of North Carolina. Fourth, we are closely identified with Governor Hodges."[16]

The nonprofit status turns out to be the key that unlocks a lot of doors. Business people now see less risk of losing investment, as government can now help fund vital missing infrastructure, and some donations are tax deductible. Hodges and other government officials see it as a firewall against self-dealing and corruption, one to which they can contribute state funds without seeming to favor one corporation over another. The universities don't cross into commercial territory that might compromise their essential teaching mission or present conflicts of interest for faculty researchers. And just as significant, the nonprofit status signals that the park is meant to benefit the common good of the whole state—accountable to its citizens, not shareholders—just as Davis envisioned.[17]

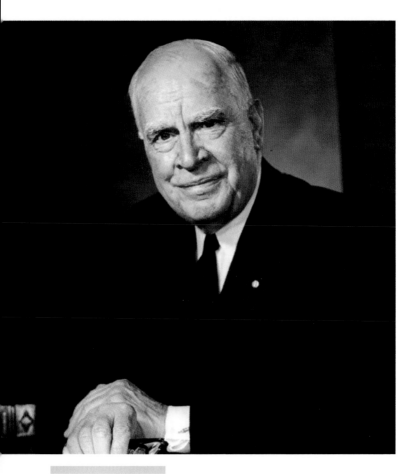

Support from Luther Hodges, who served as governor of North Carolina from 1954 to 1961, was integral to putting plans for Research Triangle Park into motion. Hodges called RTP "the heart and the hope of North Carolina's industrial future."

Subcommittees chaired by university professors help to cement the private-public collaboration. Later, handpicked university faculty serve as recruiters, contacting companies and pitching the park as an incubator of new ideas and new technologies.

RTP's boosters need something concrete to sell, so they buy the first tracts of land, four thousand acres midway between Raleigh and Durham, convenient to both the Southern Railway and two major highways, NC 54 and US 70A. The land is mostly farms and pine forest and costs just $175 per acre.[18]

One of the faculty recruiters is William Little, a chemistry professor at UNC Chapel Hill. He and others convince the Chemstrand Corporation—an Alabama synthetic fiber manufacturer that plans to build its main research facility in Princeton, New Jersey—to locate it instead at the Park. Chemstrand becomes the first anchor, acquiring one hundred acres for laboratories totaling two hundred thousand square feet and employing four hundred scientists, technicians, and administrators. Its modern two-story brick-and-glass laboratory wing, fronting on a broad green lawn, would look right at home on any university campus.

The U.S. Forestry Service builds another laboratory. The Research Triangle Institute employs a hundred researchers in two buildings. One, the Camille Dreyfus Memorial Laboratory, focuses on basic research into polymers, supported by a $2.5 million grant from the Dreyfus Foundation. Soon those operations are joined by the Environmental Protection Agency (EPA), International Business Machines (IBM), the Burroughs Wellcome Company, and the National Institute of Environmental Health Sciences Center.[19]

Research Triangle Park is very much a *park*—low-rise laboratory campuses spaced out among acres of pine and hardwood forest, parking lots softened by wide lawns, connected by a network of scenic, curving roads and wide, straight highways, in the gentle hills of the Piedmont.

Research Triangle Park is soon the largest establishment of its kind in the country, five thousand acres and growing, home to scores of companies large and small and thousands of employees, managed by the Research Triangle Foundation, a nonprofit with the mission of developing the Park into a technological hub. RTP begins to redefine not just the Triangle metro area but the entire state as one that is no longer stuck in nineteenth-century industries.[20]

Romeo Guest's assistant, Phyllis Branch, later writes, "No doubt there were others besides Mr. Guest and Dr. Odum who thought the general proximity of three great universities might someday result in a great potential force, but I think the record is perfectly clear that it was Mr. Guest who not only named Research Triangle and who did the early thinking about how it might work [but also] found a group of people to give it life's blood, and the spank which gave it birth."[21]

Odum and Guest saw different facets of the same grand vision—and others came to share that vision and shape it: Governor Hodges, Archie Davis, William Friday, George Simpson—and a roster of dozens more who raised or contributed funds, crafted legislation, secured new tenants, proposed avenues for research, and designed and managed the various parts of the enterprise. After countless meetings, planning sessions, arguments, and years of steady work, the three sides of the triangle have joined, a vision now become reality, mapped into North Carolina's future.

Visitors came to "the miracle on Morgan Street" to view works purchased with the state's original $1 million appropriation, as well as seventy-one pieces gifted by the Kress Foundation, including paintings by Veronese and Tintoretto.

CHAPTER

THE **ART** OF
THE **IMPOSSIBLE**

O n the day after Christmas 1951, a gray-haired self-made
millionaire and art collector from New York named Carl W.
Hamilton knocks on the door of a stranger's home in southern
California. He bears two suitcases heavy with photographs of
two hundred paintings chosen for purchase by the North Carolina State Art Commission—five men appointed by Governor
W. Kerr Scott—as the core of a public collection for exhibit in a
state-owned museum in Raleigh.

The stranger he seeks is Wilhelm Reinhold Valentiner, a
German-born American art historian and collector. He is the
director-consultant of the Los Angeles County Museum of Art
and soon to play the same role at the Getty Museum in Malibu.
Valentiner is widely considered the preeminent art museum
director of his generation—perhaps of the twentieth century.
Hamilton is seeking his expert opinion: Should the commission
spend $1 million on the paintings?

Under the Greenwood (1881) by George Inness; *Vanitas Flower Still Life* (circa 1656–1657) by Willem van Aelst; *A Tough Story* (1886) by John George Brown; *Capricco: The Rialto Bridge and the Church of S. Giorgio Maggiore* (circa 1750) by Canaletto (Giovanni Antonio Canal); "*Fiercely the red sun descending/Burned his way along the heavens*" (1875–1876) by Thomas Moran.

Valentiner is seventy-one years old, lean and balding, near the end of a long and distinguished career that began at the Metropolitan Museum of Art in New York and, after he returned to Germany for army service in the First World War, continued at the Kaiser Friedrich Museum in Berlin. Later he directed the Detroit Institute of Arts for two decades. He knows North Carolina's reputation as a tobacco producer. "But [Raleigh] certainly was not known as an art center," he later writes. "I was amazed to learn that the State of N.C. had appropriated one million dollars, not for a museum building, as is usually the start of a museum in American cities, but for the acquisition of a collection of paintings of old masters."[1]

Valentiner approves of most of the paintings on the list, impressed that a group of four amateurs and one art historian has compiled such a strong catalogue. Those 157 paintings by Dutch, Flemish, French, Italian, German, Spanish, British, and

American artists become the germ of a permanent collection designed to cover the breadth of artistic achievement in the Western tradition. Valentiner faults the commission for not including works by modern artists—not even Impressionists—considered "heinous" by the state attorney general. The collection is conservative, noncontroversial, heavily Eurocentric. Even American masters are mostly shunned as too provincial for a museum meant to elevate the cultural experience of all citizens.[2]

But Valentiner is right to marvel at the state appropriation—the first time any state has ever funded a public art collection.

Like the collection, the effort to form a state art museum has its own provenance, dating at least to 1924, when the Fine Arts Society formed with the eventual aim of acquiring and exhibiting a public collection of great art. From the start, the goal was to make inspiring art accessible to all citizens, to enrich civic life and culture by nurturing an appreciation for beauty. Prominent citizens such as Katherine Pendleton Arrington and Clarence Poe, the editor of the *Progressive Farmer*, lent their influence to the effort. Three years later, incorporated as the North Carolina State Art Society under its first president, John J. Blair, it staged art programs and small, temporary exhibits in spaces provided under charter with the state government.

Through a magazine article, the Art Society attracted the interest of an elderly, wealthy businessman from Cabarrus County, then living in New York: Robert Fulenwider Phifer. Phifer, an amateur painter, had accumulated a large collection of art. Keen to find it a permanent home for public viewing, he wrote his friend Blair, who arranged for an exhibition at the 1927 North Carolina State Fair. The following year, Phifer passed away at a sanatorium in Battle Creek, Michigan, bequeathing seventy-five paintings of varying worth to the Art Society. In his final weeks, he wrote, "I feel now that any pictures I may leave the Art Society will be properly shown."

More significantly—and surprisingly—the terms of his will named the Art Society as a beneficiary of an estate trust worth more than $1 million, should the original four family beneficiaries leave no heirs. Eventually the entire trust, along with significant interest, does revert to the Art Society, creating a permanent endowment for the purchase of art works.[3]

The Great Depression stalled any momentum toward a permanent museum, though New Deal programs hired some local artists and federal funds were used for art competitions. In 1943, pursuing an energetic progressive agenda even in the middle of war, Governor J. Melville Broughton established the Citizens Committee for a State Art Gallery, appointing as its head Robert Lee Humber, a hard-charging international lawyer and art connoisseur from Greenville. Humber took on the challenge and proved adept at the politics of fundraising. He informed the legislature that he had secured a one-million-dollar pledge from an anonymous donor, calling on them to match it.

On April 4, 1947—with just one day left in the legislative session—State Representative John Kerr Jr. of Warren County championed the appropriations bill, declaring, "Mr. Speaker, I know that I am facing a hostile audience, but man cannot live by bread alone." He urged his colleagues to do "the far-sighted, statesmanlike thing without being afraid."[4]

Thus S.B. 395 passed the House by three votes before passing the Senate. It contained two important provisos: First, the money would be made available only when it had been determined that the state had a budget surplus to cover it. Second, no money would be released until the matching gift of $1 million was in the bank.[5]

The first proved to be no problem, but the second nearly derailed the project. Humber's pledge was a verbal agreement with Samuel H. Kress, the five-and-dime magnate who'd used his fortune to acquire one of the world's most important collections of Italian Renaissance artwork. But the Kress Foundation, charged with distributing the assets, had no record of the pledge—and Samuel Kress was too ill to manage his own affairs.

The Kress Foundation—which was planning to distribute its vast collection to eighteen selected museums across the United States, with its flagship donation of five hundred pieces going to the National Gallery of Art—proposes an alternative. It offers Raleigh a million dollars' worth of exquisite art.

The state money buys such works as *The Armorer's Shop* (circa 1640–1645), a rare composite painting. The Flemish painter David Teniers the Younger is credited with creating the smoky gray ambience of the workshop, where bent figures in red shirts labor over dark blades, while a small section in the foreground, attributed to Jan Brueghel the Younger, features a pile of assorted armor rendered in such fine detail it seems to have a steely weight. And *Madonna and Child in a Landscape* (circa 1496–1499) by the Italian painter Giovanni Battista Cima da Conegliano, in which mother and child are haloed by a clouded blue sky and behind them folds a textured blanket of brown hills limned by a golden horizon.

With funds from the Phifer bequest—initially $300,000—the commissioners purchase *St. Jerome in His Study* (circa 1440), attributed to the German master Stefan Lochner. The saint, who famously translated the Bible from Hebrew and Greek into Latin, is shown robed in red, leaning away from his reading desk, the small dark space fractured by shafts of rectangular sunlight emanating from narrow upright windows. The Phifer funds also acquire several portraits by John Singleton Copley, an eighteenth-century American painter who lived in London and is noted for painting such revolutionary figures as Samuel Adams and Paul Revere.

NCMA's early collection was curated to highlight artistic achievements
in the Western tradition, including the *Peruzzi Altarpiece* by Giotto,
Sir William Pepperrell (1746–1816) and His Family by John Singleton
Copley, and *St. Jerome in His Study* by Stefan Lochner.

The Kress Foundation furnishes seventy-one paintings and sculptures, including such works as *Young Man with a Sword* (circa 1633–1645) by the Circle of Rembrandt van Rijn, the muted browns of the subject's cloak and umber background set off by the luminous rosy flesh of his face, a hint of a smile on his lips.

The gem of the collection—the *Peruzzi Altarpiece* (circa 1310–1315) of Giotto di Bondone and his assistants—comes from the Kress Foundation in 1960 by way of the National Gallery, which reputedly declines to accept the piece because of its horizontal format. The altarpiece is composed of five steepled panels painted with tempera and gold leaf, depicting Christ in the middle;

Art historian Wilhelm Reinhold Valentiner became the first director of the North Carolina Museum of Art in 1955.

his mother, Mary, at his right hand; and three other saints: St. John the Evangelist, St. John the Baptist, and St. Francis of Assisi. It was possibly painted for the Peruzzi family chapel in the Franciscan church of S. Croce in Florence. Its importance lies partly in the work itself—a rare, complete, surviving Giotto altarpiece, and the only one outside Europe.

But it is also the work of Giotto—considered by some art historians to be one of the most influential artists who ever lived. He revolutionized the flat Byzantine style and presented his figures in a more human manner, three-dimensional, with recognizable facial expressions and signature gestures. For those art historians, Giotto signals the beginning of the Italian Renaissance.[6]

In 1955, the Commission persuades Valentiner to come out of retirement to head the new museum, and he proves to be an inspired—and inspiring—choice. Though in poor health, partially deaf, now divorced and living alone, both eccentric and somewhat bemused to be living in such a provincial town as Raleigh, he immediately sets a professional tone for the museum. His initial staff is small: James Byrnes, associate director; Benjamin Williams, curator of exhibitions and a UNC graduate; and May Davis Hill, librarian, registrar, and curator of prints—along with enthusiastic volunteers.[7]

With little social life, Valentiner gives the museum his whole focus—it becomes the thing that keeps him going. "You ask me if I am happy in Raleigh?" he writes to his former assistant at the Getty, Mary Adams. "The working conditions are better than in Los Angeles, but there is little fun in this provincial town where no restaurant or even drugstore is open after nine and the only bookstore with a few decent books is the Museum."[8]

As a director who is also a curator and scholarly historian, Valentiner establishes high standards for both showing the work in a coherent way—according to schools based on nations and periods—and researching the provenance of the works and the history of the various schools of painting. He himself writes the catalog for the North Carolina Museum of Art (NCMA) collection, founds a journal of art history, publishes prolifically in other scholarly journals, and remains tireless in his devotion to the art. He seems energized by the prospect of building a world-class gallery from scratch, in a most unlikely place. He writes, "It is one of the pleasures of life to work oneself up again and again."[9]

He curates loan exhibitions, enlarging the experience of the museum and attracting patrons for repeat visits to see the newest works. Almost immediately, he begins cultivating out-of-state donors and searching out new additions to the permanent collections during his summer trips to Europe, acquiring Egyptian, Greek, and Roman art, along with textiles and sculpture.

Hamilton and Humber remain active as board members and advisers, and Valentiner often finds them vexing, at times exasperating. Both are zealous in their Protestant religion and preach in their spare time, Humber as a Methodist and Hamilton as an independent—and Valentiner is a secularist. Both are strong, opinionated personalities. Humber in particular is used to being in charge. At one point, Valentiner writes a letter threatening to resign, but he neither mails it nor throws it away.[10]

One bone of contention is the gallery space itself—the musty old Highway Division building on Morgan Street, intended as a temporary home until a more permanent site can be found. Valentiner wants a modernist building. The other two want to create a Beaux-Arts aura—and they win out. Thus the plain supporting columns of the old building are sheathed in black marble, the drab walls are hung with tapestries, and the entrance is embellished with a limestone classical portal.

Governor Luther Hodges cuts the ribbon on opening day, April 6, 1956, and as imperfect as the physical museum is, from the start, the public loves it. For the city of Raleigh, NCMA is a point of civic pride. For others, it signals the realization of a democratic dream of making fine art available to every citizen. Generations of school kids grow up in its corridors, gazing at the old masters, dreaming of making their own art. Newspapers call it "the miracle on Morgan Street."[11]

The museum opened on Morgan Street in 1956, and its limestone portal regularly saw deliveries from the Railway Express Agency—the FedEx of its day.

Whatever his differences with Humber and Hamilton, Valentiner recognizes their achievement, at least in a backhanded way. He writes in his unpublished memoirs, "This is the story of the creation of the Raleigh state museum, which turned out to be a popular success. It is mostly due to the initial work of the two personalities, Hamilton and Humber. The extraordinary part is that they together produced a fine museum with an excellent collection though they knew very little about art." They relied, he says accurately, on the expertise of consultants and dealers. And adds, enigmatically, that "other personal motivations played a much greater part in their work than love of art."[12]

At last, the unflagging work of many dedicated art lovers, businesspeople, politicians, and volunteers over the course of decades, channeled and focused by the premier museum director of his age, have combined to make a seemingly impossible dream come true: the great art of the world now has a lasting home in North Carolina, a state that has declared by its actions and its purse a sense of cultural aspiration, that art matters, that an appreciation of beauty makes better citizens.

When Governor W. Kerr Scott
appeared on the January 17, 1953,
cover of *Our State* magazine—then
called *The State*—as "North Carolinian
of 1952," he wore his signature
accessories: a cigar in his hand, a smile
on his face, and a red rose in his lapel.

CHAPTER

THE **SQUIRE** OF **HAW RIVER**

North Carolina enters the postwar decade in a tumult of aggressive politics, pitting old-guard heavyweights against upstart progressives. The crisis of war is over, and with it the focus on the war effort at the expense of other programs. There's a lot to be done—for businesses, schools, roads, and social needs—and robust arguments about what should be done first and at what cost, and how it should be paid for.

Out of the hurly-burly of politics emerges a dark horse, a leader of bold vision and plain speaking, a dairy farmer from Alamance County named William Kerr Scott. He goes by Kerr (pronounced "Car"), fitting for a man who will become famous for building roads.

Scott is a farmer's son, born on April 17, 1896—before the turn of the twentieth century, before the rise of automobiles and the invention of the first successful airplane, before the Great Depression and two world wars. He builds his own home and dairy farm less than a mile from the farmstead where he was born, the sixth of eleven children, to Robert W. "Farmer Bob" and Elizabeth Hughes Scott. "Farmer Bob" was actually politically sophisticated: he served on the State Commission of Agriculture under seven governors, hosted Governor Charles B. Aycock in his home on several occasions, and was a two-term state senator and five-term representative.

His son has inherited his political savvy. Kerr Scott is a devoted Presbyterian, a lifelong student of the Bible, and also a pragmatist with vision, who can see not just an ideal future but also what is possible in the here and now. Politics is the art of the possible, and he is gifted with the ability to make more things possible. He is impatient with the ruling powers, which to him are unquestionably concentrated in the cities and favor big business over the needs of the common people—rural people. In conversation, he is deeply attentive, but he speaks his mind—directly, even bluntly, though always with an old-fashioned courteousness.

He has a sturdy farmer's build, curly dark hair often worn swept back from his high forehead, and thick eyebrows that give his smile a boyish, mischievous look. He is equally at home in a pinstriped three-piece suit or denim overalls and a straw hat.

As the state commissioner of agriculture for a dozen years, he has earned a legendary reputation for knowledge and competence.

In 1948, he sets his sights on the governorship. Among other politicians, he inspires either fierce loyalty or total enmity, rarely anything in between. But his real constituency is made up of ordinary people, on farms and in small towns. He becomes their champion. In an impassioned speech in Asheville, just three days before resigning as commissioner of agriculture and formally announcing his bid for governor, he advocates for significantly extending rural phone and electric service, improving rural schools, and undertaking a massive project to pave farm-to-market roads.

He calls his daring program "Go Forward with Scott." His critics warn that his grand spending program will bankrupt the state. His backers call him "Squire."

"'The Squire of Haw River' is still a good listener, a deep student of what he hears and reads; and then, when he makes up his mind what should be done and how it should be done, he goes out and does it," writes Robert Redwine, his biographer, introducing a volume of his speeches and letters—many of them responses to the more than three hundred thousand letters sent to him by citizens.[1]

Scott's credo is simple and persuasive: "What is bad for any large segment or group of the people is bad for all the people."[2]

At the turn of the previous decade, in 1940, Senator Furnifold Simmons—architect of white supremacy policy for the "Redeemer" Democrats since the turn of the century—passed away at eighty-six. That same year, J. Melville Broughton, a Raleigh attorney, succeeded to the governor's mansion, ushering in a new era of cautiously progressive, wartime government.

But in the span of little more than a decade, the political arena has been rocked by a series of unexpected deaths of some of the most prominent standard-bearers of government—including a governor and five sitting, elected senators—three of them also former governors.

Having finished the one term as governor allowed by law, Broughton was elected to fill the unexpired term of Senator Josiah Bailey (who died four years into his third term)—over the interim appointee, William B. Umstead. Then, at the age of sixty, and just three months into his term, Broughton died of heart failure. In a move that surprised many observers, the governor appointed Frank Porter Graham, the president of the

University of North Carolina and an unabashed liberal, to fill the unexpired term.

But when he stands for the special election in 1950, he is ambushed by his opponent in the primary runoff, Willis Smith, one-time speaker of the State House of Representatives, by a series of racially charged campaign ads created by his publicity team: attorneys Bill Joyner and Tom Ellis; Hoover Adams, a newspaper publisher from Dunn; and the news director for WRAL TV, Jesse Helms.

"Did *YOU* know? Over 28% of the population of North Carolina is COLORED?" reads one campaign flyer. "THE SOUTHERN WORKING MAN MUST NOT BE SACRIFICED to *vote-getting ambitions of political bosses*!" In other words, a vote for Graham will be a vote for "Negro domination"—an old white supremacist trope right out of the Furnifold Simmons era. Another ad features a photo of racial mingling—Black soldiers and white English women dancing together during the war. The implication is clear: Graham's liberal policies would lead to interracial marriage—so-called miscegenation.

Graham loses the seat. Smith himself dies in office in 1953 at age sixty-six.

So the political landscape is littered with casualties when Kerr Scott takes the field.

In these days of one-party Democratic supremacy, the primary—not the general election—is decisive. Scott's gubernatorial opponents are R. Mayne Albright, a liberal war veteran running as an anti-machine candidate; and Charles Johnson, the state treasurer, endorsed by the party's establishment, including a majority of legislators. Former speaker of the house Thomas Pearsall serves as Johnson's campaign manager.

Johnson edges out Scott in the three-way primary by fewer than nine thousand votes, but Scott campaigns on toward the

After winning the governorship with his "Go-Forward" campaign,
Scott participated in the Forsyth County Centennial Celebration
in May 1949—a grand event that included a pageant and a parade
that rolled down West Fourth Street in Winston-Salem.

runoff brilliantly, connecting with people around the state with his down-to-earth manner, tailoring to local audiences his folksy anecdotes that illustrate the problems of bad roads and poor schools. Scott attracts the backing of progressives such as Terry Sanford, a Fayetteville attorney and future governor. In the runoff, Scott picks up most of the Albright faction and wallops Johnson by almost thirty-five thousand votes, carrying sixty-five counties—a clear and stunning mandate. He enjoys especially vigorous support in rural counties, and his most ardent supporters style themselves "the branch head boys"—referring to those who live far up the creeks or "branches" and away from towns. In the general election, he carries 73 percent of the vote—nearly 112,000 more votes than those won in the state by Harry Truman, who ran at the top of the ticket.[3]

As governor, Scott is as good as his word, shaking up the status quo. He appoints the first woman to the Superior Court, Susie Sharp, then goes on to appoint more women to boards and commissions than any previous governor. Though he has remained committed to segregation, he appoints the first Black man ever to serve on the State Board of Education: Dr. Harold Leonard Trigg, former president of Elizabeth City State Teacher's College and current president of St. Augustine's College. To his critics, he responds, "Comprising almost one-third of the population of our state, and with 30 percent of the children attending public schools being their children, the Negro race is entitled to and should have representation on the Board of Education." Scott's progressive ideas are vigorously opposed by a group of hardcore conservative legislators who caucus after hours and call themselves the "Hold-the-Liners."[4]

Limited by state law to a single term, in just four years, Scott accomplishes an amazing record of achievement: 14,810 miles of new roads and highways, which is more than was paved in all the decades before his inauguration; 8,000 new classrooms, 175 new gymnasiums, and 350 lunchrooms in public schools; an annual appropriation of $550,000 to fund a health program in the public schools; and more than $300 million of capital improvements in state colleges and universities and hospitals serving patients afflicted with tuberculosis and mental impairment, as well as general community hospitals—4,406 new beds in 77 hospitals serving 73 of the 100 counties, some of which have not previously had a hospital at all. Under Scott's administration, the deepwater ports of Wilmington and Morehead City come online at a cost of $7.5 million. Remarkably, he accomplishes all of this by raising only one tax: a penny per gallon of gas to fund roads—and leaves the state treasury with a surplus of $40 million—which gives him special pleasure, having been accused of attempting to bankrupt the state with overambitious plans. In the private sector, nearly 400 new industrial plants have been built, employing some 40,000 workers with a payroll approaching $100 million. And in keeping with his promise to make life better for the "branch head" folks, they now enjoy more than 30,000 new telephone and more than 150,000 new electric connections.[5]

In his farewell radio address on December 30, 1952, Governor Scott reminds his audience of his guiding philosophy: "The people are sovereign. When the shouting and tumult is over, their expressed verdict always prevails. Oftentimes the thinking of the people is far ahead of their political leaders. This has been demonstrated time and time again." He goes on, citing the statistic that just one-third of North Carolinians live in cities; the other two-thirds constitute "an impoverished, mud-tax afflicted, rural population [that] makes poor customers for any trading center or metropolitan area." He continues, "I became a candidate for governor because of these two convictions—that rural

North Carolina was a land of forgotten people, and that what is bad for two-thirds of the people is bad for all." As he nears the finale of his speech, "the end of the row that we have been ploughing together for the past four years," his voice breaks, falters to a near whisper, before regaining vigor and volume. "I shall not live in the past," he promises. "May the God of us all be with you and North Carolina forever."[6]

True to his word, his eyes on the future, in 1954 he successfully campaigns to unseat Alton Lennon and fill the unfinished term of Senator Willis Smith. It was Smith with his vicious racial attacks who unseated Senator Graham—who in turn was appointed by Governor Scott. Now the political wheel has come full circle.

In 1954, while running for U.S. Senate, Scott (second from right) described walking twenty-one miles in six hours and promised a bull calf to anyone who could beat his time. Forty walkers participated in a footrace; thirty-six—including the winner, Paul "Hardrock" Simpson (right)—took home a calf.

That same year, Senator Clyde Roark Hoey, a staunch opponent of Roosevelt's New Deal—aged fifty-seven—dies four years into his third term, and Sam Ervin begins a twenty-year tenure in the seat.

Meanwhile, William B. Umstead—once unseated from the U.S. Senate by J. Melville Broughton—succeeds Scott as governor. Two days after his inauguration, Umstead suffers a heart attack, is hospitalized, and remains bedridden for more than four months. In October 1954, a severe cold turns to pneumonia, and on November 7, he dies of congestive heart failure. Lieutenant Governor Luther H. Hodges, a principled, conservative businessman, serves out the remaining two years of Umstead's term and wins election to a full term of his own. Hodges operates on the theory that "the sound principles of good business could and should apply to government." He titles his political memoir, *Businessman in the State House.*[7]

In the U.S. Senate, Scott continues his progressive agenda on a larger scale. Championing a world food bank to ease the suffering of millions of starving people around the globe, he testifies, "Well-fed and well-clothed masses of people cling to their freedoms, fight for increased dignities for the individual, and never succumb to the false promises and siren songs of the Frankenstiens who fashion the creeds of shadowy isms."[8]

At home for Easter vacation in 1958, Scott suffers a heart attack and is taken to Alamance County General Hospital in Burlington, where his doctors expect him to recover. But he takes a sudden bad turn and dies on April 16, 1958, the day before his sixty-second birthday.[9]

At his Senate memorial session, Senator Lyndon B. Johnson of Texas says, "Kerr Scott loved people. Kerr Scott's love was not an abstract, academic love. He wanted to do things for them because he was one of them. And they responded in full measure to his devotion."[10]

The Carolina States of Durham strikes a note played by many newspapers in the wake of his unexpected death. In "A Great Loss to North Carolina" the editors write, "This newspaper did not always agree with Kerr Scott. In fact there were times when we disagreed with him most vehemently and took him to task in these columns. But Kerr Scott was a big enough man with whom one might disagree without having to suffer subsequent reprisals at his hand. He was no yes, yes man and did not like such around him. . . . Only a strong man can have power in his hands and not use it to destroy those who are weak."[11]

The *Greensboro Record* says simply, "Kerr Scott had faith in the people and the people had faith in him."[12]

Perhaps the most eloquent eulogy comes from the *Winston-Salem Journal*: "Kerr Scott is dead. And yet he lives. In every nook and corner of North Carolina stand monuments to his life and handiwork. Every rural school, nearly every farm home, has in some way felt the influence of this simple but blunt-speaking man whose life and character so clearly exemplified the official motto of this state: *Esse Quam Videri*—To be rather than to seem."[13]

CODA

The 1950s has been a decade of speed, of postwar exuberance, and of impatience with the slow pace of change—in politics, in economic fortunes, in cultural habits, and especially in racial justice. Out of that roiling, restless ambition has emerged a New North State, with a declared commitment to art, opportunity, and justice. Going forward—fast.

ACKNOWLEDGMENTS

I am indebted to Elizabeth Hudson (Editor in Chief), Todd Dulaney (Executive Editor), Bernard Mann (President and Publisher), Katie Saintsing (Associate Editor), Katie King (Editorial Assistant), and Jason Chenier (Art Director) at *Our State* for their important roles in imagining the original Decades series and making it a reality, and to Julia Ellis for careful and laborious fact-checking. I am extremely grateful also to Lynn York and Robin Miura at Blair, whose enthusiasm and hard work shaped the book project into something special and lasting. And none of the stories in this volume would be possible without the tireless support and assistance of my wife, Jill Gerard, who accompanied me on many of my adventures into the colorful and eventful 1950s.

I am also grateful for the help of other individuals who lent their time and expertise to the project:

Rebecca A. Baugnon, Library Specialist at William Madison Randall Library Special Collections, University of North Carolina Wilmington

John Coffey, Deputy Director for Collections and Research, the North Carolina Museum of Art

Kat Harding, Public Relations Manager, the North Carolina Museum of Art

Lyle Humphrey, Associate Curator of European Art, the North Carolina Museum of Art

Ann Freeman

William Freeman

Robert T. Patterson

John Swaine, CEO of the International Civil Rights Museum in Greensboro

Rebecca Taylor, Manager of the Federal Point History Center

PHOTOGRAPHY CREDITS

COVER

Left. Photo by Margaret Bourke-White/The LIFE Picture Collection/
Shutterstock

Center. Governor W. Kerr Scott, courtesy of Hugh Morton Photographs and
Films, Wilson Special Collections Library, UNC-Chapel Hill

Right. Courtesy of the *News & Observer*

PRELUDE

Page 2. Courtesy of Hugh Morton Photographs and Films, Wilson Special
Collections Library, UNC-Chapel Hill

Page 3. Courtesy of Hugh Morton Photographs and Films, Wilson Special
Collections Library, UNC-Chapel Hill

CHAPTER 1

Page 10. Photo by Margaret Bourke-White/The LIFE Picture Collection/
Shutterstock

Page 13. Courtesy of Cape Fear Museum of History and Science,
Wilmington, NC

Page 15. Courtesy of Cape Fear Museum of History and Science,
Wilmington, NC

CHAPTER 2

Page 20. Courtesy of the State Archives of North Carolina

Page 24. Courtesy of the *News & Observer*

Page 27. All courtesy of the *News & Observer*

Page 30. Courtesy of the *News & Observer*

CHAPTER 3

Page 32. Courtesy of Warren Colloway

Page 39. Courtesy of Cape Fear Museum of History and Science, Wilmington,
NC

Page 42. Courtesy of the Wilmington Railroad Museum

CHAPTER 4

Page 44. Courtesy of ClassicStock / Alamy Stock Photo

Page 46. Courtesy of the State Archives of North Carolina

Page 51, top. Courtesy of the University of North Carolina at Chapel Hill
    Photographic Laboratory Collection, Wilson Library, UNC-Chapel Hill

Page 51, bottom. Courtesy of the State Archives of North Carolina

CHAPTER 5

Page 54, top. Courtesy of Hugh Morton Photographs and Films, Wilson
    Special Collections Library, UNC-Chapel Hill

Page 54, inset. Courtesy of Hugh Morton Photographs and Films, Wilson
    Special Collections Library, UNC-Chapel Hill

Page 61. Courtesy of Hugh Morton Photographs and Films, Wilson Special
    Collections Library, UNC-Chapel Hill

Page 63, both photos. Courtesy of Hugh Morton Photographs and Films,
    Wilson Special Collections Library, UNC-Chapel Hill

CHAPTER 6

Page 66. Courtesy of Davidson County Historical Museum, Lexington, NC /
    H. Lee Waters Photography Collection

Page 73, top. Courtesy of the *Charlotte Observer* Photograph Collection
    (Robinson-Spangler Carolina Room, Charlotte Mecklenburg Library)

Page 73, bottom. Courtesy of the *Greensboro News & Record*

Page 75. Courtesy of the *Greensboro News & Record*

CHAPTER 7

Page 78. Courtesy of Forsyth County Public Library Photograph Collection,
    Winston-Salem, NC

Page 82. Courtesy of Piedmont Aviation Historical Society

Page 87. Courtesy of Piedmont Aviation Historical Society

CHAPTER 8

Page 90. © Andrew Craft – USA TODAY NETWORK

Page 95. Courtesy of the State Archives of North Carolina

Page 96. Courtesy of Mary Livermore Library, University Archives/Special
    Collections, University of North Carolina at Pembroke, Pembroke, NC

Page 97, both photos. Courtesy of Mary Livermore Library, University
    Archives/Special Collections, University of North Carolina at Pembroke,
    Pembroke, NC

CHAPTER 9

Page 100. Courtesy of RTI via Wikicommons

Page 103. Courtesy of the Portrait Collection, Wilson Library, UNC-Chapel Hill

Page 108. Courtesy of Hugh Morton Photographs and Films, Wilson Special Collections Library, UNC-Chapel Hill

CHAPTER 10

Page 112. Courtesy of the State Archives of North Carolina

Page 114, all images. Courtesy of the North Carolina Museum of Art, Raleigh

Page 115. Courtesy of the North Carolina Museum of Art, Raleigh

Page 119, top. Courtesy of the State Archives of North Carolina

Page 119, bottom left and bottom right. Courtesy of the North Carolina Museum of Art, Raleigh

Page 120. Courtesy of the North Carolina Museum of Art, Raleigh

Page 123. Courtesy of the North Carolina Museum of Art, Raleigh

CHAPTER 11

Page 126. Courtesy of Hugh Morton Photographs and Films, Wilson Special Collections Library, UNC-Chapel Hill

Page 131, campaign button. Courtesy of the North Carolina Museum of History, Raleigh

Page 131, parade photo. Courtesy of Forsyth County Public Library Photograph Collection, Winston-Salem, NC

Page 134. Courtesy of the State Archives of North Carolina

NOTES

PRELUDE

1. Alexander, "Even with No Major League Team," *Baseball Reference*, https://www.baseball-reference.com/bullpen/Piedmont_League; "Chrome and Color: Cars of the 1950s," and "Passenger Color Options for 1954," https://studebakersocal.com/RayLin_ColorCharts.htm; "Now Playing: Drive-Ins in North Carolina"; Stern, "The Fast Food Explosion of the 1950s—When It Was Cool!"; and "Char-Grill" (1959).
2. "History of Grandfather Mtn," https://grandfather.com/about-grandfather-mountain/history-of-the-mountain/.
3. Kennedy, "Atlantic Coast Line Railroad."
4. Turner, "Piedmont Airlines 'Flies the Blue Skies.'"
5. Taylor, "Seabreeze Part 6—The 50s."
6. "Highlights in NC State History."
7. McKinney, *Greater Freedom*, 74.
8. Akshay Gupta, "Annotated Timeline of the Civil Rights Movement in North Carolina," "Senator Sam Ervin and the 1964 Civil Rights Act"; Dr. Flora Bryant Brown, "African American Civil Rights in North Carolina."
9. "History and Culture."
10. Graham, "Lumbee Indians Face the Ku Klux Klan, 1958."
11. PBS North Carolina, "About PBS North Carolina: The History of PBS North Carolina (formerly UNC-TV)," http://www.unctv.org/about/history/.
12. North Carolina Museum of Art, "History of the Museum."
13. Williams, "Research Triangle Park."
14. Troxler, "Go-Forward Program."

CHAPTER 1

1. Kahrl, *The Land Was Ours*, 155–56.
2. Taylor, "Seabreeze—A History Part 1—The Freeman Family."
3. Kahrl, *The Land Was Ours*, 157.
4. Taylor, "Seabreeze Part 3—With the Turn of the Century"; Kahrl, *The Land Was Ours*, 161.
5. Kahrl, *The Land Was Ours*, 158–59.
6. Taylor, "Seabreeze—A History Part 2—Carolina Beach and Shell Island."

7. Taylor, "Seabreeze Part 5—The 40s."

8. Hook, "Oral History—Fessa' John Hook—'Jim Hannah, One of the Two Original Beach Music Pioneers' "; "Genre Spotlight: Carolina Beach."

9. Hook, "Oral History."

10. Taylor, "Seabreeze Part 6—The 50s"; Kahrl, *The Land Was Ours*, 171.

11. Shakur, "Memories of Seabreeze."

12. Taylor, "Seabreeze Part 6—The 50s."

13. "Hurricane Hazel, October 15, 1954"; note: Taylor, "Seabreeze Part 6—The 50s," cites an eighteen-foot surge, which was recorded by the National Weather Service in Calabash, just south. Twelve feet is probably a conservative estimate.

14. Taylor, "Seabreeze Part 6—The 50s."

15. Kahrl, *The Land Was Ours*, 175.

16. Bower, "Our Coast: A Shelter During Segregation."

CHAPTER 2

1. *Carteret County News-Times*, May 19, 1950, 2.

2. *Carteret County News-Times*, May 19, 1950, 3–4.

3. Godfrey, "1950s Prices."

4. Godfrey, "1950s Prices"; Lefler and Newsome, *North Carolina*, 639.

5. Lefler and Newsome, *North Carolina*, 650–51.

6. My Aunt Helen and Uncle Whitey drove a spruce-green Buick, and my dad bought a 1959 Wedgewood blue Ford station wagon because my mom liked the color.

7. Stone, "Father of Drive-Ins Says 'Never Again,' " *Motion Picture Herald*, Jan. 28, 1950, 38, cited in Segrave, *Drive-In Theaters*, Ch. 1: "A Backyard Invention" (no page numbers in ebook).

8. Stone, "Father of Drive-Ins Says 'Never Again," 38, cited in Segrave, *Drive-In Theaters*.

9. Segrave, *Drive-In Theaters*, cited in Ch. 1: "A Backyard Invention" (no page numbers in ebook); prices from newspaper advertisement for Camden drive-in.

10. "Eden Drive-In," http://cinematreasures.org/theaters/9953; patronage figure cited in Segrave, *Drive-In Theaters*, Ch. 7: "The Golden Years, 1950s," and "Appendix 6: Number of Drive-ins, by state" (no page numbers in ebook).

11. "Raleigh Road Outdoor Theatre"; and "*Ali Baba and the Forty Thieves* (1944)."

12. Cited in Segrave, *Drive-In Theaters*, Ch. 7: "The Golden Years, 1950s" (no page numbers in ebook).

13. Segrave, *Drive-In Theaters*, Ch. 7 (no page numbers in ebook).

14. Details about the invention and early years of drive-ins at "The Drive-In Theater History Page," and "The History of Drive-In Movie Theaters (and Where They Are Now)"; "First Drive-In Movie Opens," https://www .history.com/this-day-in-history/first-drive-in-movie-theater-opens; and "The Golden Years: Selling Food," in Segrave, *Drive-In Theaters* (no page numbers in ebook).

15. "Eden Drive-In," http://cinematreasures.org/theaters/9953; Segrave, *Drive-In Theaters*, Ch. 7, "The Golden Years, 1950s" (no page numbers in ebook).

16. Staton, "How Many Drive-In Movie Theaters Were in Wilmington?"; "Bessemer City Kings Mountain Drive-In"; Conner, "Badin Road Drive-In"; "Thunderbird Drive-In"; Leah, "Hidden History: North Carolina's Lost Drive-In Theaters," https://abc11.com/community-events/ hidden-history-north-carolinas-lost-drive-in-theaters/4175275/.

17. "Starlite Drive-In."

18. Segrave, *Drive-In Theaters*, Ch. 7: "The Golden Years, 1950s" (no page numbers in ebook).

19. Jessiebeth Brady Geddie, interview by the author.

20. Steelman, "In Its Day, Mil-Jo Drive-In Was the Place to Be."

21. "A True Carolina Treasure."

22. "10 Retro Places in North Carolina That Will Take You Back in Time."

23. Bledsoe, "The Story of Hardee's."

CHAPTER 3

1. "Passenger Deficit 'Staggering,' " *Railway Age*, Nov. 22, 1954, 8–10 (cited in Alcorn, "Between the Lines").

2. Alcorn, "Between the Lines," 24; Alcorn cites three sources from *Railway Age*.

3. Burns, "ACL's Florida Special," https://www.american-rails.com/flda- spcl.html (site features separate pages for each train). Title page of sheet music on display at the Wilmington Railroad Museum.

4. Population statistic from U.S. Department of Commerce, "1950 Census of Population, Preliminary Counts," https://www2.census.gov/library/ publications/decennial/1950/pc-02/pc-2-10.pdf; ACL number from

Steelman, "MyReporter Shares the History of Railroad Powerhouse Champ Davis."

5. Alcorn, "Between the Lines," 20; Alcorn cites "Pullman's Vicious Ad" from *Aviation Week*, June 26, 1950, 54.

6. Details of the wrecks from Haine, *Railroad Wrecks*, 112–14; "This Date in History, Dec. 16: Atlantic Coast Line Rail Crash Kills 74"; "Train Collision in Stockton, GA"; Interstate Commerce Commission, "Investigation No. 2751, the Atlantic Coast Line Railroad Company Report in RE Accident Near Rennert, N.C., on December 16, 1943."

7. Steelman, "Railroad Powerhouse Champ Davis" and Cameron Museum of Art, "Claude Howell Timeline."

8. From menu of the Palmetto Limited, Wilmington Railroad Museum.

9. Menu card on display at the Wilmington Railroad Museum.

10. Gannon, "A Long Wait's Ahead before Passenger Rail Service Returns to Area," *Wilmington Star News*, June 15, 2008, https://www .starnewsonline.com/news/20080615/a-long-waits-ahead-before-passenger-rail-service-returns-to-area.

CHAPTER 4

1. "WUNC-TV Re-Slated for Operation Starting Jan. 8"; "Formal TV Dedication Held with Chancellors."

2. "About PBS North Carolina: The History of PBS North Carolina (formerly UNC-TV)"; Chansky, *Light Blue Reign*, 297–98; "WUNC-TV to Receive $10,000 Gift Today."

3. Link, *William Friday*, 28–29; also cited in "About PBS North Carolina."

4. "Formal TV Dedication Held with Chancellors"; Murrow, "The 1951 Introduction to 'This I Believe.' "

5. "About PBS North Carolina."

6. "About PBS North Carolina."

7. "About PBS North Carolina"; United States District Court, W.D., North Carolina, Charlotte Division (McMillan, District Judge), "Jefferson Standard Broadcasting Company v. F.C.C."

8. Career details for Kay Kyser also from Beasley, "Kay Kyser, the Ol' Professor of Swing"; Link, *William Friday*, 189.

9. Friday's progressive ethic discussed in Link, *William Friday*, vi.

10. "About PBS North Carolina."

11. "Brighter TV in Education Stressed Here."

12. "WUNC-TV Returns to Air After Four-Week Vacation."

13. The workshop details and quotes from Grimes, "WUNC-TV Workshop Make Learning Fun."

14. *Fieldcrest Mill Whistle*, "Smithfield Supervisors Take Course on TV."

15. King, "Bill Friday Never Forgot His Black and Gold Roots."

16. "WUNC-TV Schedule."

17. "About PBS North Carolina"; McNichol, "William Friday Dies on University Day at 92."

CHAPTER 5

1. Steelman, "Who Is Hugh Morton?"

2. "Hugh Morton" (obituary): "He wants to be remembered as the guardian of Grandfather Mountain," said his daughter, Catherine Morton.

3. "History of Grandfather Mtn."

4. Later recalibrated at 5,282 feet and new sign erected in 1999 when the steel bridge replaced the wooden one.

5. "Mile-High Swing Bridge Dedicated."

6. Tager, *Grandfather Mountain*, 64. *Tanawha* (*Tanawwha* in Dugger's glossary) is variously translated as "fabulous hawk" or "fabulous eagle," and the Grandfather Mountain audio tour calls it "fabulous hawk."

7. Tager, *Grandfather Mountain*, vi, 3. The official height of Grandfather Mountain at the Linville Peak summit is 5,946, though other sources say 5,945 or 5,964, the latter based on a 1917 survey, now corrected. Grandfather Mountain Stewardship Foundation, "Grandfather Mountain, North Carolina: Wonders Never Cease," track 4, "Sphinx and Split Rocks."

8. Tager, *Grandfather Mountain*, 8; also "Grandfather Mountain, North Carolina: Wonders Never Cease," track 3, "On the Way to Sphinx and Split Rocks," and track 10, "Mile-High Swinging Bridge."

9. Tager, *Grandfather Mountain*, 29–30.

10. Bent, "Safe in the Arms of Grandfather" (reprinted from Bent, "Mountain's 'children' face extinction," *Watauga Democrat*, June 5, 1995, pp. 1A, 2A); and Grandfather Mountain Stewardship Foundation, "Grandfather Mountain, North Carolina: Wonders Never Cease," track 2, "Picnic Area," and track 3, "On the Way to Sphinx and Split Rocks."

11. Tager, *Grandfather Mountain*, 8.

12. Tager, *Grandfather Mountain*, 53, 57–58; Michael Hardy, "The Sestercentennial Death of the Linvilles."

13. Tager, *Grandfather Mountain*, 74.

14. "History of Grandfather Mtn," https://grandfather.com/about-grandfather-mountain/history-of-the-mountain/modern-history/.

15. Tager, *Grandfather Mountain*, 31–32.

16. Tager, *Grandfather Mountain*, 87–90.

17. Tager, *Grandfather Mountain*, 94–97.

18. "History of Grandfather Mtn."

19. The author's personal experience, as related in his notebook from his recent visit, augmented by earlier descriptions of the wooden bridge on the audio tour. The steel bridge emits high-pitched shrieks from time to time, metal on metal, as it too moves, and the wind sings through the cable just as described on the audio tour—sounding like a harmonica.

CHAPTER 6

1. Patterson quotes and other details, including the abortive attempt on Jan. 31, from Robert T. Patterson, interview.

2. Momodu, "Greensboro Sit-Ins (1960)."

3. From a photograph in "Separate Is Not Equal: Brown v. Board of Education."

4. McCain quotes from Norris, "The Woolworth Sit-In That Launched a Movement" (transcript), Feb. 1, 2008, https://www.npr.org/templates/story/story.php?storyId=18615556.

5. McKinney, *Greater Freedom: The Evolution of the Civil Rights Struggle in Wilson, North Carolina*, 10.

6. Brown, "The 1946 Case of the 'Last Mass Lynching in America.' "

7. Details of President Truman's Civil Rights activities from Brown, "How Harry S. Truman Went from Being a Racist to Desegregating the Military"; Leuchtenburg, "The Conversion of Harry Truman."

8. Account of Marie Everett's arrest and trial from McKinney, *Greater Freedom*, 8, 14–17.

9. Akshay Gupta, "Annotated Timeline of the Civil Rights Movement in North Carolina," "Senator Sam Ervin and the 1964 Civil Rights Act."

10. "History—Brown v. Board of Education Re-enactment," https://www.uscourts.gov/educational-resources/educational-activities/history-brown-v-board-education-re-enactment.

11. McKinney, *Greater Freedom*, 72–73.

12. Marable, *Race, Reform, and Rebellion*, 43.

13. "Report of the North Carolina Advisory Committee on Education," April 5, 1956, https://digital.ncdcr.gov/digital/collection/p16062coll17/id/247/.

14. Thuesen, "Pearsall Plan," *Encyclopedia of North Carolina*, edited by William S. Powell (Chapel Hill: University of North Carolina Press, 2006), in NCPedia, https://www.ncpedia.org/pearsall-plan.

15. Account and McCain quotes from Norris, "The Woolworth Sit-In That Launched a Movement"; Momodu, "Greensboro Sit-Ins (1960)"; additional quotes and details, such as McCain's ROTC uniform, from Robert T. Patterson, interview.

CHAPTER 7

1. Details of Runser and Turner's visit from Eller, *Piedmont Airlines*, Ch. 1: "Winston-Salem Air, 1918–1944"; "Aviation."

2. Davis, *The History of Piedmont* (quoted in Eller, *Piedmont Airlines*, Ch. 1).

3. Eller, *Piedmont Airlines*, Ch. 1: "Winston-Salem Air, 1918–1944; "Aviation."

4. Yardley, "Money and Murder in the Old South."

5. Price, "Puddle Jumper Piedmont on Last Leg," *Raleigh News & Observer*, July 16, 1989, p. 31A (quoted in Eller, *Piedmont Airlines*).

6. Davis, *The History of Piedmont* (quoted in Eller, *Piedmont Airlines*).

7. Ortlepp and Fellow, "The Desegregation of Airports in the American South."

8. Piedmont Airlines Newsletter, Aug. 21, 1948, in North Carolina Newspapers, http://newspapers.digitalnc.org/lccn/2014236869/1948-08-21/ed-1/.

9. Piedmont Airlines Newsletter, Dec. 22, 1948, in North Carolina Newspapers, http://newspapers.digitalnc.org/lccn/2014236869/1948-12-22/ed-1/.

10. Eller, *Piedmont Airlines*, Ch. 6: "The Hazards of Flight, 1959–1988."

11. Eller, *Piedmont Airlines*, Ch. 6: "The Hazards of Flight, 1959–1988."

12. "Investigations Begun in Death of Bridegroom."

13. Details of crash and investigation from Eller, *Piedmont Airlines*, Ch. 6: "The Hazards of Flight, 1959–1988," which cites CAB report; and Railey, "Survivor Recalls Piedmont Air Crash 50 Years Ago."

CHAPTER 8

1. Dial and Eliades, *The Only Land I Know*, 30–31.

2. Bryant and LaFramboise, "The Racial Identity and Cultural Orientation of Lumbee American Indian High School Students," 82–89.

3. Stilling, "Introduction to the Lumbee," and "Chronology of Significant Events in the History of Robeson County Indians."

4. Mitchell, "Lowry Band."

5. This and subsequent quotations from Verdia Locklear from her interview for the Museum of the Southeast American Indian at UNC Pembroke, Aug. 13, 2018, https://www.youtube.com/watch?v=6NZWSaGNYGA.

6. "Bad Medicine for the Klan"; Dial and Eliades, *The Only Land I Know*, 160.

7. "Bad Medicine for the Klan."

8. Dial and Eliades, *The Only Land I Know*, 160.

9. "The Battle of Maxton Field."

10. Stilling, "Chronology of Significant Events."

CHAPTER 9

1. Abbott, "North Carolina's Research Triangle Park"; Link, *William Friday: Power, Purpose, and American Higher Education*, 56, 77.

2. Rohe, *The Research Triangle*, 63.

3. Williams, "Research Triangle Park."

4. Letter to W. B. Hamilton, quoted in Abbott, "North Carolina's Research Triangle Park: A Success Story of Private Industry Fostering Public Investment to Create a Homegrown Commercial Park," 575.

5. Memo to Phyllis Branch, Nov. 5, 1954, in RGP, box 10, Advertising and Related Correspondence 1954, p. 1; quoted in Alex Sayf Cummings, " 'Brain Magnet': Research Triangle Park and the Origins of the Creative City, 1953–1965."

6. Abbott, "North Carolina's Research Triangle Park," 457.

7. Quoted in Abbott, "North Carolina's Research Triangle Park," 578.

8. Abbott, "North Carolina's Research Triangle Park," 574–75; Hill, "Luther Hartwell Hodges: Governor, 1954–1961."

9. Lefler and Newsome, *North Carolina*, 691.

10. Quoted in Rohe, *The Research Triangle*, 63.

11. Rohe, *The Research Triangle*, 63; Cummings, " 'Brain Magnet.' "

12. Rohe, *The Research Triangle*, 68.

13. Link, *William Friday*, 212–13.

14. Abbott, "North Carolina's Research Triangle Park," 585–87, 594.

15. Lefler and Newsome, *North Carolina*, 690.

16. Letter from George L. Simpson Jr., Dir., The Research Triangle Comm., Inc., to Karl Robbins (May 10, 1957), in the Romeo Guest Papers, quoted

in Abbott, "North Carolina's Research Triangle Park," 588.

17. Abbott, "North Carolina's Research Triangle Park," 582–83.
18. Rohe, *The Research Triangle*, 67.
19. Lefler and Newsome, *North Carolina*, 691; Rohe, *The Research Triangle*, 71–72.
20. Lefler and Newsome, *North Carolina*, 691, as of 1961—now 7,000 acres.
21. Letter to Dr. Louis R. Wilson, Professor at UNC, quoted in Abbott, "North Carolina's Research Triangle Park," 573.

CHAPTER 10

1. Cotten, "Valentiner, William Reinhold"; Humphrey, "Saul Among the Prophets," 10–11.
2. Humphrey (p. 12) describes the number of purchases, including costs of each. See also North Carolina Museum of Art, *Catalogue of Paintings Including Three Sets of Tapestries*.
3. Crute, "Phifer, Robert Fulenwider."
4. *North Carolina Museum of Art: A Brief History* (pamphlet for thirtieth anniversary 1956–1986), NC Department of Cultural Resources, 1986.
5. Kirby, *The North Carolina Museum of Art: The First Fifty Years, 1947–1997, a Selected Chronology*, Appendix: "General Assembly, Act of 1947."
6. The information about the paintings comes from the NCMA labels (author's photographs), and the descriptions are my own, based on personal observation.
7. John Coffey, interview.
8. Quoted in Humphrey, "Saul Among the Prophets," from the Mary E. Adams letters in the Archives of American Art, Smithsonian Institution, Washington, DC; her footnote 37.
9. Quoted in Humphrey, "Saul Among the Prophets," her footnote 38.
10. Coffey and Humphrey interviews. Coffey also described the granite sheathing and tapestries, which he saw as a boy while visiting the galleries.
11. *North Carolina Museum of Art: A Brief History*.
12. Quoted in Humphrey, "Saul Among the Prophets," her footnote 69.

CHAPTER 11

1. Corbitt (ed.), *Public Letters and Papers of William Kerr Scott, Governor of North Carolina, 1949–1953*, ix–x.
2. Corbitt, *Public Letters and Papers of William Kerr Scott*, xiii.

3. Eamon, *The Making of a Southern Democracy*, 18–21.

4. Corbitt, *Public Letters and Papers of William Kerr Scott*, xxii.

5. Corbitt, *Public Letters and Papers of William Kerr Scott*, xxiii–xxiv

6. "A Governor's Last Look," Dec. 30, 1952, cited in Corbitt, *Public Letters and Papers of William Kerr Scott*, 327–28.

7. Hodges, *Businessman in the Statehouse*, 5.

8. According to Sen. Hubert Humphrey, cited in United States Congress, *William Kerr Scott*, 57.

9. According to Sen. Sam Ervin, cited in United States Congress, *William Kerr Scott*, 23.

10. United States Congress, *William Kerr Scott*, 16.

11. *Carolina States* (Durham, NC), April 26, 1958, cited in United States Congress, *William Kerr Scott*, 120.

12. Dec. 17, 1958, cited in United States Congress, *William Kerr Scott*, 128.

13. April 18, 1958, cited in United States Congress, *William Kerr Scott*, 156.

SELECTED SOURCES

ARTICLES

"10 Retro Places in North Carolina That Will Take You Back in Time." Only in Your State, Sept. 26, 2015. https://www.onlyinyourstate.com/north-carolina/retro-places-nc/.

Abbott, Morgan P. "North Carolina's Research Triangle Park: A Success Story of Private Industry Fostering Public Investment to Create a Homegrown Commercial Park." 40 *Campbell Law Review* 569 (2018).

"About PBS North Carolina: The History of PBS North Carolina (formerly UNC-TV)." PBS North Carolina. http://www.unctv.org/about/history/.

Alexander, Chip. "Even with No Major League Team, NC Is Home to Baseball History." *Raleigh News & Observer*, July 1–3, 2016. http://www.newsobserver.com/sports/mlb/article87307212.html.

"*Ali Baba and the Forty Thieves* (1944)." IMDb. https://www.imdb.com/title/tt0036591/.

Aronica, Molly. "Where Your Favorite Fast-food Chains Began." *USA Today*, May 31, 2014. https://www.usatoday.com/story/travel/destinations/2014/05/31/fast-food-chains-origins/9729901/.

"Aviation." Reynolda. https://reynolda.oncell.com/en/aviation-179832.html.

"Bad Medicine for the Klan." *Life* magazine, Jan. 27, 1958, pp. 26–28.

"The Battle of Maxton Field." North Carolina Department of Cultural Resources. Jan. 11, 2019. https://www.ncdcr.gov/blog/2019/01/09/battle-maxton-field.

Beasley, Steven. "Kay Kyser, the Ol' Professor of Swing." Excerpted from *Back in the Mood* magazine. https://www.kaykyser.net/kay.html.

Bent, Jennifer. "Safe in the Arms of Grandfather." *Appalachian Journal* 23, no. 1 (Fall 1995): 21–22 (Jennifer Bent, "Mountain's 'Children' Face Extinction," *Watauga Democrat*, June 5, 1995, 1A, 2A).

"Bessemer City Kings Mountain Drive-In." *Cinema Treasures.* http://cinematreasures.org/theaters/29440/photos/112627.

"Better Buy Buick" advertisement. *Carteret County News-Times* at Digital North Carolina project. http://newspapers.digitalnc.org/lccn/sn94058246/1950-05-19/ed-1/seq-2/#date1=1950&index=2&date2=1950&sequence=0&lccn=sn94058246&rows=20&words=&dateFilterType=yearRange&page=1.

Bledsoe, Jerry. "The Story of Hardee's." *Our State*, May 27, 2011. https://www
.ourstate.com/hardees/.

Bordsen, John. "10 Secrets Grandfather Mountain Never Told You." *Charlotte
Observer*, April 8, 2016. https://www.charlotteobserver.com/living/
travel/article70565567.html.

Bower, Jennifer. "Our Coast: A Shelter During Segregation." *Coastal Review*.
https://www.coastalreview.org/2015/09/our-coast-seabreeze/.

"A Brief History of Car Colors—And Why Are We so Boring Now?"
Consumerist, May 4, 2018. https://www.consumerreports.org/
consumerist/a-brief-history-of-car-colors-and-why-are-we-so-boring-
now/.

"Brighter TV in Education Stressed Here." *Daily Tar Heel*, Feb. 5, 1955, p. 1.
http://newspapers.digitalnc.org/lccn/sn92073228/1955-02-05/ed-1/
seq-1/#date1=02%2F05%2F1955&index=0&date2=02%2F05%2F1955
&sequence=1&lccn=sn92073227&lccn=sn92073228&lccn=sn92068245
&lccn=sn92073230&rows=20&words=&dateFilterType=range&page=1.

Brown, DeNeen L. "How Harry S. Truman Went from Being a Racist to
Desegregating the Military." *The Washington Post*, July 26, 2018.
https://www.washingtonpost.com/news/retropolis/wp/2018/07/26/
how-harry-s-truman-went-from-being-a-racist-to-desegregating-the-
military/?utm_term=.98e8d5261128.

———. "The 1946 Case of the 'Last Mass Lynching in America.'" *The
Washington Post*, Feb. 12, 2019. https://www.heraldnet.com/nation-
world/the-1946-case-of-the-last-mass-lynching-in-america/.

Brown, Flora Bryant. "African American Civil Rights in North Carolina."
NCPedia, from *Tar Heel Junior Historian*, Tar Heel Junior Historian
Association of the North Carolina Museum of History, Fall 2004.
https://www.ncpedia.org/history/20th-Century/african-american-civil-
rights.

Bryant, Alfred Jr., and Teresa D. LaFramboise. "The Racial Identity and
Cultural Orientation of Lumbee American Indian High School
Students." *Cultural Diversity and Ethnic Minority Psychology* 11, no. 1
(2005): 82–89. http://test.scripts.psu.edu/students/s/e/seb302/bryant_
laframboise.pdf.

Byrd, Robert L. "Smith, Willis." *Dictionary of North Carolina Biography*,
edited by William S. Powell. Chapel Hill: University of North Carolina
Press, 1979–1996. https://www.ncpedia.org/biography/smith-willis.

Caldwell, Martha B. "Carmichael, William Donald, Jr." *Dictionary of*

North Carolina Biography, edited by William S. Powell. Chapel Hill: University of North Carolina Press, 1979–1996. https://www.ncpedia .org/biography/carmichael-william-dona-0.

Cameron Museum of Art. "Claude Howell Timeline." https://www.tiki-toki .com/timeline/entry/393449/Claude-Howell-TImeline/.

"Char-Grill (1959)." VisitRaleigh. https://www.visitraleigh.com/plan-a-trip/ visitraleigh-insider-blog/post/institutions-the-oldest-restaurants-in- raleigh-nc/.

Chavers, Dan. "Battle of Hayes Pond: The Day Lumbees Ran the Klan Out of North Carolina." *Indian Country Today*, Jan. 18, 2017. https:// newsmaven.io/indiancountrytoday/archive/battle-of-hayes-pond- the-day-lumbees-ran-the-klan-out-of-north-carolina-RN9W5- vIJUKsXc6TqZWO9g/.

"Chrome and Color: Cars of the 1950s." *Taste Washington Travel*, Oct. 3, 2016.

Conner, Tammy. "Badin Road Drive-In." *Cinema Treasures*. http:// cinematreasures.org/theaters/3269.

"Consolidated University Television Will Start This Afternoon at 5:28." *Daily Tar Heel*, Jan. 8, 1955, p. 1.

Cotten, Alice R. "Valentiner, William Reinhold." *Dictionary of North Carolina Biography*, edited by William S. Powell. Chapel Hill: University of North Carolina Press, 1979–1996. https://www.ncpedia.org/biography/ valentiner-william.

Crute, Adair Phifer. "Phifer, Robert Fulenwider." *Dictionary of North Carolina Biography*, edited by William S. Powell. Chapel Hill: University of North Carolina Press, 1979–1996. https://www.ncpedia .org/biography/phifer-robert-fulenwider.

Cummings, Alex Sayf. " 'Brain Magnet': Research Triangle Park and the Origins of the Creative City, 1953–1965." *Journal of Urban History*, Nov. 3, 2015.

Davis, Tom. "Devotion to the People: The Legacy of Helen Scheirbeck." *Tribal College Journal of American Indian Higher Education* 12, no. 4 (Summer 2001). https://tribalcollegejournal.org/devotion-people- legacy-helen-scheirbeck/.

"Formal TV Dedication Held with Chancellors." *Daily Tar Heel*, Jan. 11, 1955, p. 1. https://newspapers.digitalnc.org/lccn/sn92073228/1955-01-11/ ed-1/seq-1/.

Gatton, T. Harry. "Hoey, Clyde Roark." *Dictionary of North Carolina*

Biography, edited by William S. Powell. Chapel Hill: University of North Carolina Press, 1979–1996. https://www.ncpedia.org/biography/ hoey-clyde-roark.

"Genre Spotlight: Carolina Beach." Southern Museum of Music. http://www.southernmuseumofmusic.com/Spotlight/01-Genre/ Carolina-Beach.htm.

Godfrey, Andrew. "1950s Prices." *Nostalgia and Now*. Jan. 6, 2010. https:// nostalgia049.wordpress.com/2010/01/06/1950s-prices/.

Graham, Nicholas. "Lumbee Indians Face the Ku Klux Klan, 1958." NCPedia, from "This Month in North Carolina History," UNC–North Carolina Collection, 2005. https://www.ncpedia.org/history/20th-Century/ lumbee-face-klan.

"Grandfather Mountain." *Winston-Salem Journal*, Oct. 5, 2008, p. A18.

Greaves, Brendan, and M. C. Taylor. "Beach Music: History and Myth." South Writ Large—Stories, Arts, and Ideas from the Global South. https:// southwritlarge.com/articles/fooled-around-and-fell-in-love-beach- music-history-and-myth/.

Grimes, Mary Edna. "WUNC-TV Workshop Make Learning Fun." *The (Meredith College) Twig*, March 16, 1956. http://newspapers.digitalnc .org/lccn/2015236797/1956-03-16/ed-1/seq-4/#index=0&rows=20&pro xtext=WUNC+TV&searchType=basic&sequence=0&words=TV+WUNC +WUNC-TV&page=1.

Hardy, Michael. "The Sestercentennial of the Death of the Linvilles." *Avery Journal Times*, July 27, 2016. https://www.averyjournal.com/ news/community/the-sestercentennial-of-the-death-of-the-linvilles/ article_8a15abcc-3fe5-5192-bd2a-c0630ed7fae8.html.

Henlon, Leigh Ann. "The History of Grandfather Mountain's Mile High Swinging Bridge." *Our State*, Oct. 2010. https://www.ourstate.com/ grandfather-mountain-bridge-history/.

"Highlights in NC State History." NC State University Libraries. https://historicalstate.lib.ncsu.edu/timelines/highlights-in-nc-state- history.

Hill, Michael. "Luther Hartwell Hodges: Governor 1954–1961." Research Branch, NC Office of Archives and History, 2001. NCPedia. https:// www.ncpedia.org/biography/governors/hodges.

"History and Culture." Lumbee Tribe of North Carolina. http://www .lumbeetribe.com/history-culture.

"The History of Drive-In Movie Theaters (and Where They Are Now." New

York Film Academy. June 7, 2017. https://www.nyfa.edu/student-resources/the-history-of-drive-in-movie-theaters-and-where-they-are-now/.

"History of Grandfather Mtn." Grandfather Mountain. https://grandfather.com/about-grandfather-mountain/history-of-the-mountain/.

"History of the Museum." North Carolina Museum of Art. https://ncartmuseum.org/about/history/.

Hook, John. Oral History—Fessa' John Hook—"Jim Hannah, One of the Two Original Beach Music Pioneers," from Fessa' John Hook's oral history, "Jim Hannah, One of the Two Original Beach Music Pioneers, 1920–2010." *Dancing on the Edge Journal* 1, no. 1 (Feb. 8, 2010). http://federal-point-history.org/fphps-news/oral-history-fessa-john-hook-jim-hannah-one-of-the-two-original-beach-music-pioneers/.

"Hugh Morton" (obituary). *Charlotte Observer*, June 2, 2006. https://www.legacy.com/obituaries/charlotte/obituary.aspx?n=Hugh-Morton&pid=17964593.

Huler, Scott. "The Man and Plan Behind Research Triangle Park." *Our State*, Aug. 25, 2014. https://www.ourstate.com/research-triangle-park/.

Humphrey, Lyle. "Saul Among the Prophets: W. R. Valentiner, Robert L. Humber, Carl W. Hamilton, and the Italian Collection at the NCMA." *Collecting Early Modern Art (1400–1800) in the U.S. South*, edited by Lisandra Estevez. Newcastle upon Tyne, UK: Cambridge Scholars Publishing, 2021. https://www.cambridgescholars.com/resources/pdfs/978-1-5275-6365-0-sample.pdf.

"Hurricane Hazel, October 15, 1954." National Weather Service. https://www.weather.gov/mhx/Oct151954EventReview.

"Investigations Begun in Death of Bridegroom." AP report in the *Monroe (La.) News-Star*, June 14, 1956. https://newspaperarchive.com/monroe-news-star-jun-14-1956-p-1/Ortlepp.

James, Phil. "Fiftieth Anniversary: The Final Flight of Piedmont Airlines 349." *Crozet Gazette*, Oct. 13, 2009. https://www.crozetgazette.com/2009/10/13/secrets-of-the-blue-ridge-the-fiftieth-anniversary-of-the-final-flight-of-piedmont-349/.

Jenkins, Jay. "How the Amateur Lobbyist Got $1,000,000 for Art." *The State*, Jan. 1984.

Kennedy, George A. "Atlantic Coast Line Railroad." NCPedia, 2006, from the *Encyclopedia of North Carolina*, edited by William S. Powell. Chapel

Hill: University of North Carolina Press, 2006. https://www.ncpedia
.org/atlantic-coast-line-railroad.

King, Kerry M. "Bill Friday Never Forgot His Black and Gold Roots." *Wake
Forest Magazine*, Oct. 12, 2012. https://magazine.wfu.edu/2012/10/12/
former-unc-president-bill-friday-dies/.

"Lanier to Ask Anti-Klan Laws; Klavern Slated Here—Panther." *Daily
Tar Heel*, Jan. 7, 1950, p. 1. https://newspapers.digitalnc.org/lccn/
sn92073228/1950-01-07/ed-1/.

Leah, Heather. "Hidden History: North Carolina's Lost Drive-In Theaters."
ABC 11, Sept. 7, 2018. https://abc11.com/community-events/hidden-
history-north-carolinas-lost-drive-in-theaters/4175275/.

Leonard, Teresa. "Glory Days of Rail Travel in NC Were Gone by the 1950s."
*News & Observe*r online. https://www.newsobserver.com/living/liv-
columns-blogs/past-times/article43267848.html.

Leuchtenburg, William E. "The Conversion of Harry Truman." *American
Heritage* 42, no. 7 (Nov. 1991). https://www.americanheritage.com/
conversion-harry-truman.

Link, Albert N., and John T. Scott. "The Growth of Research Triangle Park."
Small Business Economics 20, no. 2, Special Issue on Policies Promoting
Innovation in Small Firms (March 2003): 167–75.

Maupin, Armistead Jones. "North Carolina Museum of Art." *Encyclopedia of
North Carolina*, edited by William S. Powell. Chapel Hill: University of
North Carolina Press, 2006. https://www.ncpedia.org/north-carolina-
museum-art.

"McCain, Franklin (Franklin Eugene), 1941–." Civil Rights Digital Library.
http://crdl.usg.edu/people/m/mccain_franklin_franklin_eugene_1941/
and http://crdl.usg.edu/people/m/mccain_franklin_franklin_
eugene_1941/.

———. "McNeil, Joseph (Joseph Alfred), 1942–." http://crdl.usg.edu/
people/m/mcneil_joseph_joseph_alfred_1942/?Welcome.

McNichol, Beth. "William Friday Dies on University Day at 92." UNC Alumni
News. https://alumni.unc.edu/news/william-friday-dies-on-university-
day-at-92/.

"Mile-High Swinging Bridge Dedicated": NC DNR, Sept. 2, 2016. https://
www.ncdcr.gov/blog/2016/09/02/mile-high-swinging-bridge-
dedicated.

Mitchell, Thornton W. "Lowry Band." *Encyclopedia of North Carolina*, edited by William S. Powell. Chapel Hill: University of North Carolina Press, 2006. https://www.ncpedia.org/lowry-band.

Momodu, Samuel. "Greensboro Sit-Ins (1960)." *Black Past.* https://www .blackpast.org/african-american-history/greensboro-sit-ins-1960/.

Morgan, Phil. "Trailblazer Tributes: William Linville." *Blue Ridge Outdoors*, Nov. 16, 2017. https://www.blueridgeoutdoors.com/go-outside/ trailblazer-tributes-william-linville/.

Morgan, Thomas S. "Cherry, Robert Gregg." *Dictionary of North Carolina Biography*, edited by William S. Powell. Chapel Hill: University of North Carolina Press, 1979–1996. https://www.ncpedia.org/biography/ cherry-robert-gregg.

Murrow, Edward R. "The 1951 Introduction to 'This I Believe.' " National Public Radio, April 4, 2005. https://www.npr.org/templates/story/story .php?storyId=4566554.

Ortlepp, Anke, and Verville Fellow. "The Desegregation of Airports in the American South." National Air and Space Museum. https://airandspace .si.edu/stories/editorial/desegregation-airports-american-south.

Osment, Timothy. "Tweetsie Railroad." https://digitalheritage.org/2010/08/ tweetsie-railroad/.

"Passenger Color Options for 1954." https://studebakersocal.com/RayLin_ ColorCharts.htm.

Powell, William S. "Kyser, James Kern ('Kay')." *Dictionary of North Carolina Biography*, edited by William S. Powell. Chapel Hill: University of North Carolina Press, 1979–1996. https://www.ncpedia.org/biography/ kyser-james-kern-kay.

Powledge, Fred. "KKK Returning to North Carolina." *Daily Tar Heel*, Nov. 1, 1956, p. 2.

Railey, John. "Survivor Recalls Piedmont Air Crash 50 Years Ago." *Winston-Salem Journal/News & Advance*, Oct. 25, 2009. https://www .newsadvance.com/news/local/survivor-recalls-piedmont-air-crash-years-ago/article_b67fd831-1160-5035-94b5-79bc19fc3b9f.html.

"Raleigh Road Outdoor Theatre." WRALcom. https://www.wral.com/ Henderson/Movies/Raleigh-Road-Outdoor-Theatre/5230675/.

"Raleigh Road Outdoor Theatre—Facts & Highlights." Drive-ins.com. https://www.driveinmovie.com/nc/henderson/raleigh-road-outdoor-theater/.

Rivers, Rob. "Many Improvements Made on Grandfather; Opens May First." *Watauga Democrat*, April 29, 1954.

Rohe, William M. *The Research Triangle: From Tobacco Road to Global Prominence*. Philadelphia: University of Pennsylvania Press, 2011.

"Sanford Locklear Discusses the 1958 Lumbee Revolt against the KKK in Maxton, NC." https://www.youtube.com/watch?v=NbikXpIRxlA.

"Scottish Clans to Celebrate Rally of 211 Years Ago." *Watauga Democrat*, Aug. 15, 1956.

"Seabreeze and Carolina Beach." Federal Point History Center. http://federal-point-history.org/history-shorts/seabreeze-and-carolina-beach/.

"Separate Is Not Equal: Brown v. Board of Education": Smithsonian National Museum of American History. http://americanhistory.si.edu/brown/history/6-legacy/freedom-struggle-2.html.

Shakur, Assata. "Memories of Seabreeze." *Assata: An Autobiography*. New York: Lawrence Hill Books, 1987. http://federal-point-history.org/carolina-beach/memories-of-seabreeze/.

Simpson, Marcus B. "Linville Gorge." *Encyclopedia of North Carolina*, edited by William S. Powell. Chapel Hill: University of North Carolina Press, 2006. https://www.ncpedia.org/linville-gorge.

"Smithfield Supervisors Take Course on TV." *The (Fieldcrest) Mill Whistle*, Jan. 1956. http://newspapers.digitalnc.org/lccn/2015236906/1966-02-07/ed-1/seq-4/#index=2&rows=20&proxtext=WUNC+TV&searchType=basic&sequence=0&words=TV+WUNC+WUNC-TV&page=1.

"Starlite Drive-In." *Cinema Treasures*. http://cinematreasures.org/theaters/24644.

Staton, John. "Cape Fear Unearthed Podcast Looks Back at Bygone Wilmington Movie Theaters and Drive-Ins." *Wilmington Star News*, June 18, 2021. https://www.starnewsonline.com/story/entertainment/2021/06/18/cape-fear-unearthed-podcast-old-wilmington-nc-movie-theaters-drive-ins/7735708002/.

Steelman, Ben. "History of Seabreeze Inspires a Call for Stories." *Wilmington StarNews* online. Nov. 10, 2014. https://www.starnewsonline.com/news/20141109/history-of-seabreeze- inspires-a-call-for-stories.

———. "In Its Day, Mil-Jo Drive-In Was the Place to Be." *Wilmington Star News* online. Feb. 22, 2010. https://www.starnewsonline.com/story/news/2010/02/22/in-its-day-mil-jo-drive-in-was-the-place-to-be/30822093007/.

———. "MyReporter Shares the History of Railroad Powerhouse Champ Davis." *Wilmington Star News*, Oct. 5, 2011. https://www.starnewsonline.com/story/news/2011/10/05/myreporter-shares-the-history-of-railroad-powerhouse-champ-davis/30874062007/.

———. "Who Is Hugh Morton?" *Wilmington Star News* online (website discontinued).

Stephens, Ronald J. "Freeman Beach-Seabreeze, Wilmington, North Carolina (ca. 1885)." Black Past. https://www.blackpast.org/african-american-history/freeman-beach-seabreeze-wilmington-north-carolina-ca-1885/.

Stern, Karl. "The Fast Food Explosion of the 1950s—When It Was Cool!" http://www.whenitwascool.com/fast-explosion-of-the-1950s/.

Stewart, A. W. "Umstead, William Bradley." *Dictionary of North Carolina Biography*, edited by William S. Powell. Chapel Hill: University of North Carolina Press, 1979–1996. https://www.ncpedia.org/biography/umstead-william-bradley.

Stilling, Glenn Ellen Starr. "Chronology of Significant Events in the History of Robeson County Indians." http://lumbee.library.appstate.edu/chronology-significant-events-history-robeson-county-indians.

———. "Introduction to the Lumbee." *Encyclopedia of North Carolina*, edited by William S. Powell. Chapel Hill: University of North Carolina Press, 2006. http://lumbee.library.appstate.edu/introduction-lumbee.

———. "Lumbee Voices: North Carolina's Lumbee Indians in Literature, Art, and Music": Lumbee History. http://lumbee.library.appstate.edu/lumbee-voices.

"Strap on the Seat Belts as Your Cyber Time Machine Takes You on a Journey to the Past." The Drive-In Theater History Page. https://www.driveintheater.com/drivhis1.htm.

Taylor, Rebecca. "Seabreeze—A History Part 1—The Freeman Family." Federal Point History Center. https://federal-point-history.org/history-shorts/seabreeze-a-history-part-i-the-freeman-family/.

———. "Seabreeze—A History Part 2—Carolina Beach and Shell Island. Federal Point History Center. https://federal-point-history.org/fphps-news/seabreeze-a-history-part-2-carolina-beach-and-shell-island/.

———. "Seabreeze Part 3—With the Turn of the Century." Federal Point History Center. https://federal-point-history.org/federal-point/seabreeze-part-3-with-the-turn-of-the-century/.

———. "Seabreeze Part 4—Growth of Seabreeze. Federal Point History Center. http://federal-point-history.org/federal-point/seabreeze-part-4-growth-of-seabreeze/.

———. "Seabreeze Part 5—The 40s." Federal Point History Center. https://federal-point-history.org/carolina-beach/seabreeze-part-5-the-40s/.

———. "Seabreeze Part 6—The 50s." Federal Point History. http://federal-point-history.org/carolina-beach/seabreeze-part-6-the-50s/.

"This Date in History, Dec. 16: Atlantic Coast Line Rail Crash Kills 74." *Wilmington Star News*, Dec. 16, 2017. https://www.starnewsonline.com/opinion/20171216/this-date-in-history-dec-16-atlantic-coast-line-rail-crash-kills-74.

"Thunderbird Drive-In." *Cinema Treasures*. http://cinematreasures.org/theaters/42757.

"Train Collision in Stockton, GA." *New York Times*, Aug. 6, 1944. https://www.rarenewspapers.com/view/590419.

"Tribe Commemorates 58th Anniversary of Battle of Hayes Pond." Lumbee Tribe of North Carolina. https://www.lumbeetribe.com/single-post/2016/1/18/Tribe-Commemorates-58th-anniversary-of-Battle-of-Hayes-Pond.

Troxler, George W. "Go-Forward Program." *Encyclopedia of North Carolina*, edited by William S. Powell. Chapel Hill: University of North Carolina Press, 2006. https://www.ncpedia.org/go-forward-program.

"A True Carolina Treasure." Short Sugars. https://shortsugars.com/.

Turner, Walter R. "Piedmont Airlines 'Flies the Blue Skies.' " NCPedia, from *Tar Heel Junior Historian*, Tar Heel Junior Historian Association of the North Carolina Museum of History, Fall 2003. https://www.ncpedia.org/aviation/piedmont-airlines.

"Twentieth Century North Carolina Timeline." North Carolina Museum of History. https://www.ncmuseumofhistory.org/learning/educators/timelines/twentieth-century-north-carolina-timeline.

Wadelington, Charles W. "Wheeler Airlines: 'An American First.' " NCPedia, from *Tar Heel Junior Historian*, Tar Heel Junior Historian Association of the North Carolina Museum of History, Fall 2003. https://www.ncpedia.org/aviation/wheeler-airlines.

Weaver, Robert. D. "Grandfather Mountain." *Encyclopedia of North Carolina*, edited by William S. Powell. Chapel Hill: University of North Carolina Press, 2006. https://www.ncpedia.org/grandfather-mountain.

"What Is Beach Music?" *Beach Music Online*. http://www.beachmusiconline.com/about/.

White, Herbert L. "Oceanside Divide." *Our State*, Nov. 3, 2013. https://www.ourstate.com/oceanside-divide/.

Williams, Wiley J. "Research Triangle Park." *Encyclopedia of North Carolina*, edited by William S. Powell. Chapel Hill: University of North Carolina

Press, 2006. https://www.ncpedia.org/research-triangle-park.

"WUNC-TV Re-Slated for Operation Starting Jan. 8." *Daily Tar Heel*, Jan. 4, 1955, p. 1.

"WUNC-TV Returns to Air after Four-Week Vacation." *Daily Tar Heel*, Sept. 23, 1956, p. 3. https://newspapers.digitalnc.org/lccn/sn92073228/1956-09-23/ed-1/seq-3/#words=air+Air+returns+Returns+TV+WUNC.

"WUNC-TV Schedule." *Daily Tar Heel*, June 20, 1960, p. 5.

WUNC-TV to Receive $10,000 Gift Today." *Daily Tar Heel*, Jan. 14, 1955, p. 1. http://newspapers.digitalnc.org/lccn/sn92073228/1955-01-14/ed-1/seq-1/#date1=01%2F14%2F1955&index=0&date2=01%2F14%2F1955&sequ ence=1&lccn=sn92073227&lccn=sn92073228&lccn=sn92068245&lccn =sn92073230&rows=20&words=&dateFilterType=range&page=1.

Yardley, Jonathan. "Money and Murder in the Old South." *The Washington Post*, Nov. 2, 1983. https://www.washingtonpost.com/archive /lifestyle/1983/11/02/money-and-murder-in-the-old-south /308cad64-1fb1-4aae-8e07-b10a4dec1a1a/.

AUDIO CD

Grandfather Mountain, North Carolina: Wonders Never Cease. The Grandfather Mountain Stewardship Foundation.

BOOKS

Chansky, Art. *Light Blue Reign: How a City Slicker, a Quiet Kansan, and a Mountain Man Built College Basketball's Longest-Lasting Dynasty.* New York: St. Martin's, 2010.

Corbitt, David Leroy (ed.). *Public Letters and Papers of William Kerr Scott, Governor of North Carolina, 1949–1953.* Raleigh: North Carolina Division of Archives and History, 1957.

———. *Public Addresses, Letters, and Papers of William Bradley Umstead.* Raleigh: North Carolina Department of Archives and History, 1957.

Davis, Thomas H. *The History of Piedmont: Setting a Special Pace.* New York: Newcomen Society of North America, 1982.

Dial, Adolph L., and David K. Eliades. *The Only Land I Know: A History of the Lumbee Indians.* Syracuse, NY: Syracuse University Press, 1996, 154–62.

Dozier, Howard D. *A History of the Atlantic Coast Line Railroad.* Boston: Houghton Mifflin, 1920; reprinted New York: Augustus M. Kelley, 1971.

Dugger, Shepherd M. *The Balsam Groves of the Grandfather Mountain: A*

Tale of the Western North Carolina Mountains. Banner Elk, NC, 1907 and 1934; originally published 1860. https://www.newrivernotes.com/topical_books_1907_balsamgroves_grandfathermountain.htm.

Eamon, Tom. *The Making of a Southern Democracy: North Carolina Politics from Kerr Scott to Pat McCrory.* Chapel Hill: University of North Carolina Press, 2014.

Eller, Richard. *Piedmont Airlines: A Complete History, 1948–1969.* Jefferson, NC: MacFarland & Company, 2008.

Haine, Edgar A. *Railroad Wrecks.* New York: Cornwall Books, 1993, 112–14.

Hodges, Luther. *Businessman in the Statehouse: Six Years as Governor of North Carolina.* Chapel Hill: University of North Carolina Press, 1962.

Ivey, A. G. *Luther H. Hodges: Practical Idealist.* Minneapolis, MN: T. S. Denison & Company, 1968.

Kahrl, Andrew W. *The Land Was Ours: African American Beaches from Jim Crow to the Sunbelt South.* Cambridge, MA: Harvard University Press, 2012.

Kirby, Peggy Jo D. *The North Carolina Museum of Art: The First Fifty Years, 1947–1997, a Selected Chronology.* Raleigh: North Carolina Museum of Art, 1997.

Lefler, Hugh Talmadge, and Albert Ray Newsome. *North Carolina: The History of a Southern State* (3rd ed.). Chapel Hill: University of North Carolina Press, 1973.

Link, William A. *William Friday: Power, Purpose, and American Higher Education.* Chapel Hill: University of North Carolina Press, 1980.

Marable, Mannings. *Race, Reform, and Rebellion: The Second Reconstruction in Black America, 1945–1990.* Jackson: University Press of Mississippi, 1984.

McKinney, Charles Wesley. *Greater Freedom: The Evolution of the Civil Rights Struggle in Wilson, North Carolina.* Lanham, MD: University Press of America, 2010.

North Carolina Museum of Art. *Catalogue of Paintings Including Three Sets of Tapestries.* Raleigh: North Carolina Museum of Art, 1956.

Pleasants, Julian. *The Political Career of W. Kerr Scott, the Squire from Haw River.* Lexington: University of Kentucky Press, 2014.

Prince, Richard E. *Atlantic Coast Line Railroad: Steam Locomotives, Ships, and History.* Bloomington: Indiana University Press, 2000.

Segrave, Kerry. *Drive-In Theaters: A History from Their Inception in 1933.* Jefferson, NC: MacFarland & Company, 1992 and 2006.

Tager, Miles. *Grandfather Mountain*. Blowing Rock, NC: Parkway
　　Publishers, 1999.

BROCHURE
"Seabreeze Beach Resort, New Hanover County, NC." Federal Point Historic
　　Preservation Society.

INTERVIEWS
Coffey, John. Deputy Director for Collections and Research, North Carolina
　　Museum of Art, by the author, July 24, 2019.
Geddie, Jessiebeth Brady, by the author, November 29, 2018, and November
　　30, 2018.
Humphrey, Lyle. Associate Curator of European Art, North Carolina
　　Museum of Art, by the author, July 24, 2019.
Locklear, Velda. UNC Pembroke video interview, August 13, 2018.
　　https://www.youtube.com/watch?v=6NZWSaGNYGA.
Patterson, Robert T., by the author, February 12, 2019.

REPORTS
Interstate Commerce Commission. "Investigation No. 2751, The Atlantic
　　Coast Line Railroad Company Report in RE Accident Near Rennert,
　　N.C., on December 16, 1943" (copy in author's possession).
United States Congress. "William Kerr Scott," in *Memorial Addresses
　　Delivered in Congress*. Washington, DC: U.S. Government Printing
　　Office, 1958.
United States Department of Agriculture. *Agricultural Statistics 1955*,
　　U.S. Government Printing Office. https://babel.hathitrust.org/cgi/
　　pt?id=osu.32435058529793;view=1up;seq=487.
United States District Court, W.D., North Carolina, Charlotte Division,
　　(McMillan, District Judge). "Jefferson Standard Broadcasting Company
　　v. F.C.C." Sept. 22, 1969. https://casetext.com/case/jefferson-standard-
　　broadcasting-company-v-fcc-3.

THESES
Alcorn, Aaron L. "Between the Lines: The Politics of Passenger Rail Service,
　　1958–1970." Master's thesis, Florida Atlantic University, August 2001.
　　http://fau.digital.flvc.org/islandora/object/fau%3A9662/datastream/
　　OBJ/view/Between_the_lines__The_politics_of_passenger_rail_
　　service__1958--1970.pdf.

Edwards, Jennifer. "A Color Line in the Sand: African American Seaside Leisure in New Hanover County, North Carolina." Master's thesis, University of North Carolina Wilmington, 2003.

WEBSITES

Hardee's. https://www.hardees.com/company/story. Piedmont Airlines archive of newsletters. http://newspapers.digitalnc.org/lccn/2014236869/1948-08-21/ed-1/seq-1/.